PERENNIALS

PERENNIALS

ALAN TOOGOOD

GALLERY BOOKS
An Imprint of W. H. Smith Publishers Inc.
112 Madison Avenue
New York City 10016

A *Macdonald Orbis* BOOK

© Macdonald & Co (Publishers) Ltd 1988

First published in Great Britain in 1988
by Macdonald & Co (Publishers) Ltd
London & Sydney

A Pergamon Press plc company

Filmset by Flair plan

Printed and bound in Portugal by Printer Portuguesa

GALLERY BOOKS
An Imprint of W. H. Smith Publishers Inc.
112 Madison Avenue
New York City 10016

INTRODUCTION

Perennials are plants which live for several to many years and have non-woody stems. A few are in fact woody at the base, but produce softer growth on this 'framework', which may well die down in the winter; these are known as sub-shrubs. A few of them will be found in this encyclopedia.

There are basically two types of perennials – herbaceous and evergreen. Most of the plants are in the former group. With herbaceous perennials the stems die down to the ground in the autumn and the plants rest as dormant 'crowns' – a cluster of growth buds, occasionally some basal leaves, and the root system. In the spring the buds start into growth, producing stems, foliage and flowers.

The evergreen perennials retain their leaves all the year round and are particularly valuable for providing greenery in the winter.

Most perennials have a normal fibrous root system (a mass of thin roots) but some have tuberous, or rather fleshy, roots. Generally these types dislike disturbance and should be handled carefully to avoid root damage. Many other perennials (as will be seen in the encyclopedia) spread by means of rhizomes, which are underground stems that grow through the soil and produce roots, stems and foliage. Rhizomes may be very thick and fleshy, as in many of the irises, or quite thin and wiry, as in some ornamental grasses.

The majority of the plants in the encyclopedia are hardy, and can survive out of doors all the year round. There are some, however, which are tender, suitable for growing out of doors only in very mild parts of the country where winters are clement. In colder areas such plants are best overwintered in a frost-free greenhouse.

USES IN THE GARDEN

Perennials have many uses and indeed are considered almost essential plants in any planting scheme, as are the shrubs. A collection of perennials is capable of providing flower colour in all four seasons, but it should be said that a very large number of them flower during the summer only.

Many people today are beginning to realize the value of foliage, which has a much longer period of interest than flowers do. There is available a wide range of perennials with attractive herbaceous or evergreen foliage and a good selection should be included in any planting scheme. Some perennials have very large, distinctive leaves; others are silver or white; and yet others have attractive variegated foliage: yellow and green, white and green, and similar combinations. The leaves of some plants are smooth and shiny; others are woolly or hairy. The foliage perennials are invaluable for creating contrasts in shape, texture and colour with flowering plants or with shrubs.

Traditionally perennials are grown in their own special bed, known as the herbaceous border. It should ideally have the backing of a dark green hedge, and be planted with tall plants at the back, becoming shorter gradually towards the front of the border, although one should not be too strict about this as the effect will be too uniform. Occasionally a group of tall plants can be brought towards the centre of the border, and some groups of shorter plants extended towards the centre.

This type of border was very popular in the nineteenth and early part of the twentieth century and then went out of favour, because it was labour-intensive (many of the plants needed some means of support). However, many of the newer perennials are self-supporting, needing minimum attention, and these are ideal candidates for a modern herbaceous border.

In a well-planned herbaceous border there will be a sprinkling of colour in the spring; this will build up gradually so that by early summer there is quite a lot of colour (from plants such as irises, lupins and peonies). In mid-summer the border should be a kaleidoscope of colour. This will fade away slowly, but autumn should by no means be devoid of colour, as then the Michaelmas daisies (asters) and a few other perennials

really come into their own. Winter should see a few plants in flower, such as winter irises and hellebores. However, it should be said that winter and early spring are the dullest times as far as the herbaceous border is concerned.

A herbaceous border looks lovely in most gardens. A more modern way of growing perennials, though, is in mixed borders, which contain all kinds of plants. The 'framework' of a mixed border is provided by shrubs (including shrub roses) – deciduous and evergreen, flowering and foliage kinds – to give colour and/or interest over all four seasons. Between and around the shrubs, contrasting in shape, colour and texture, groups of perennials as well as other plants such as bulbs can be planted. A well-planned mixed border should have something of interest all through the year.

Coming back to growing perennials on their own, a modern idea is to grow them in island beds. An island bed is an irregular-shaped bed set in a lawn (or in a paved or gravelled area). If you have the space, a group of perhaps three beds, with wide paths between them, looks most impressive.

Island beds are viewed from all sides so due regard must be taken when planning and planting them. Usually, tall plants are set in the centre, with progressively shorter plants towards the edges of the bed, so that all the plants can be seen easily. But, as with the herbaceous border, do not stick rigidly to this or the effect will be too regimented. Only self-supporting perennials are recommended for island beds as the idea is for them to be labour-saving, so avoid such plants as tall delphiniums, the tall Michaelmas daisies, etc. There are plenty of self-supporting tall plants, though, such as kniphofias, acanthus and eryngiums.

You will notice in the encyclopedia that many plants are recommended for cottage gardens. These are plants that are traditionally grown in this type of garden and

◀ *Iris pumila* Blue Denim (top), *Lupinus arboreus* (centre), and *Paeonia lactiflora* Mons. Jules Elie (bottom) will all provide the carefully thought-out herbaceuous border with much-needed colour in the early summer months. They also provide a magnificent show for the traditional cottage garden.

what today we often describe as 'old-fashioned' perennials. I have emphasized this use because cottage-style gardening is very much in vogue, even among owners of small town plots. The cottage garden is a glorious mixture of all kinds of plants: perennials, shrubs, roses, annuals and biennials, and even fruit trees, fruit bushes and vegetables.

GROWING CONDITIONS

There are perennials which are suitable for growing in any part of a garden — simply choose the most appropriate for the particular conditions. Each entry in the encyclopedia indicates the most suitable soil conditions and aspect.

Many perennials like plenty of sun and therefore such features as herbaceous beds and borders, and mixed borders, should be sited in a sunny part of the garden. However, there are numerous perennials which need, or which are suitable for, shade or partial shade. Many of these are ideal subjects for a woodland garden (if you are lucky enough to possess such a feature), or for growing in the shade of a tree or a group of shrubs.

Most perennials are very adaptable where the type of soil they are grown in is concerned, but most need well-drained conditions – in other words, soil which does not remain very wet or become waterlogged in winter. However, some plants need a moisture-retentive soil (one which does not dry out in the summer), and again there are ways of ensuring this. One or two actually need very moist or even wettish soils. These requirements are indicated in the encyclopedia.

SOIL PREPARATION

Because perennials remain where they are planted for several or many years it is important to prepare the soil thoroughly before planting, particularly if drainage or moisture retention need to be improved.

The best preparation is undoubtedly double digging, to two depths of the spade. This will certainly help to improve drainage. It involves digging out a trench 60cm (2ft) wide and the depth of the spade, across one end of the plot. Then the soil in the bottom

of this trench is forked over to the depth of the fork. Often this lower soil is very hard and compacted, which impedes drainage or surplus water. Then a second trench is dug, immediately adjacent to the first and the soil is thrown forward into the first trench. The lower soil is again broken up. Continue in this way until the plot has been dug, and fill the last trench with the soil removed from the first one.

When digging any soil it pays to incorporate bulky organic matter, like well-rotted farmyard manure, garden compost, spent hops or spent mushroom manure. Spread a layer in the bottom of each trench: about a quarter of a barrowload will be suffcient for each 1.2m (4ft) length of every trench you dig.

If drainage needs to be improved still further (for instance, if you have a heavy clay soil) then mix grit or coarse horticultural sand into the top 30cm (12 in) of soil. If the plants need a moisture-retentive soil, and you are on a very sharply drained type (such as sand or chalk) which is inclined to dry out in the summer, then add peat or leaf-mould instead. All these materials can either be forked into the top 30cm (12in) or incorporated with a rotary cultivator.

If the ground is infested with perennial weeds, then kill these off before digging by spraying them with a weedkiller containing glyphosate while they are in active growth. Follow the manufacturer's instructions.

Seven to ten days before planting, apply a general-purpose or flower-garden fertilizer and fork this into the top 5–8 cm (2–3in). Before planting, the soil should be firmed by treading and any large lumps of soil (produced by digging) should be broken down with a fork.

PLANTING PERENNIALS

Autumn or spring planting are recommended for most plants in this encyclopaedia. It should be said, however, that autumn planting is recommended only if the soil is very well drained. If it lies cold and wet over the winter then it is far better to delay planting until the spring, when the soil is drying out and warming up.

If the plants are bought in containers,

▲ *Delphiniums*, which have tall stems carrying heavy flower spikes, are almost essential subjects for the back of herbaceous borders. They should, ideally, be supported with a bamboo cane. Tie up the stems with soft garden string or raffia to prevent damage.

GENERAL CARE

It is important to keep weeds under control because they can soon choke perennials, especially dwarf or low-growing kinds, and they compete for food and moisture. Either hoe regularly in warm weather, or apply a safe weedkiller among the plants, such as the granular propachlor. Follow the manufacturer's instructions.

Many perennials will grow poorly if the soil dries out, so it may be necessary to water thoroughly and regularly in the spring and summer whenever the top 2.5cm (1in) of soil becomes dry.

Every spring apply a general-purpose or flower-garden fertilizer and hoe it lightly into the soil surface.

Mulching is a technique which suppresses the growth of annual weeds and helps to conserve soil moisture. It involves spreading a 5–8cm (2–3in) deep layer of organic matter over the soil around the plants (but not right up to the stems) in the spring. This can be peat, leaf-mould or pulverized bark. It allows you to dispense with hoeing or weedkilling, and reduces the need for watering.

Some plant need artificial supports to keep them upright. Plants with tall, thin, floppy stems can be supported with twiggy sticks inserted around them just as they are starting into growth in the spring. The stems will then grow up through the sticks and hide them. The sticks must, of course, be shorter than the ultimate heights of the plants.

Perennials that have a few tall stems which carry heavy flower spikes, especially delphiniums, can have each stem supported with a bamboo cane. Tie up the stems with very soft garden string or raffia.

Fortunately, perennials are not troubled too much by pests and diseases. Slugs and snails are, however, among the most troublesome, attacking new shoots of many plants, but especially lupins, delphiniums and hostas. Just as growth is commencing, sprinkle slug pellets around the plants. Repeat weekly, especially in wet weather.

Greenfly or aphids attack the shoot tips and leaves of many perennials, sucking the sap and severly distorting growth. As soon as you notice them, spray the plants with one of

such as pots or flexible polythene bags, then remove these carefully to avoid root disturbance and set the plants in holes slightly wider than the rootballs. Work fine soil into the space and firm it well by treading with your heels. Bare-rooted plants (including divisions – see Propagation) must have a planting hole sufficiently large to allow the roots to dangle down to their full extent. Work fine soil around them and firm well. The crown of the plant, where the buds are situated, should be at soil level after planting – on no account cover the buds with soil or they will not grow.

the modern systemic insecticides – they cannot be washed off by rain and therefore remain effective for many weeks.

Powdery mildew, which appears as a white powdery coating on shoot tips and leaves, affects some perennials, including asters or Michaelmas daisies. As soon as you notice it, spray the affected plants with a modern systemic fungicide, such as benomyl.

Cut off dead flower heads regularly from perennials (unless seeds are required or the seed heads are a particular feature) because this not only makes the bed or border look more tidy, but sometimes encourages a further flush of blooms.

When the stems of herbaceous perennials have died down in autumn, cut them down close to the crowns of the plants. Evergreen perennials should have dead leaves removed as necessary.

PROPAGATION

In the encyclopedia brief details of propagation are given, including the best time to propagate perennials. Here, the various techniques are described more fully.

Division This is the most widely used method or porpagating perennials and involves lifting and splitting the plant into a number of smaller pieces, complete with roots and buds or topgrowth. In fact, many perennials need regular lifting and dividing – about every three or four years – to keep them young and vigorous, when flowering will be very much better. There are some, though, which do not like to be disturbed, unless it is absolutely necessary; these include kniphofias, peonies, and gypsophila.

The technique is as follows. First lift the plant carefully with a fork and then shake most of the soil from the roots. If you are dealing with a very large or tough clump, then the easiest way to split it is to insert two forks, back to back, through the centre of the clump and then lever the handles apart. This results in two divisions, which can be split further by the same technique.

Many other plants, though are easily split by pulling them apart with your hands; or you may need to use a knife to cut through any

tough tissue or rhizomes.

When dividing bearded hybrid irises – those with the thick rhizomes – ensure that each division consists of a good portion of rhizome, with roots attached, plus a fan of leaves. The average size of divisions of other plants is such that they fill the palm of your hand. The centre part of a plant is discarded when dividing, because this is the oldest, and declining in vigour. Retain only the young, vigorous, outer parts for replanting.

When dividing try not to let the roots of the plants dry out and ideally replant immediately.

Cuttings The most usual type of cutting used to propagate perennials is the basal cutting. These are young shoots, about 5cm (2in) long, produced from the crown of the plant.

▼ *Kniphofias*, or red-hot pokers, can be *propagated* by dividing established clumps in spring, but they do not like to be disturbed unless necessary.

They should preferably be taken with a 'heel' of older tissue at the base, so remove them as close as possible to the crown.

The cuttings should be placed in their rooting positions before they wilt. Rooting will be speeded up by dipping the bases of the cuttings in hormone rooting powder. Then insert them in pots of cutting compost: a mixture of equal parts moist peat and coarse horticultural sand (or substitute the sand with perlite or vermiculite). Water them throughly and place them in warm humid conditions, such as an electrically heated propagating case in a greenhouse.

Some perennials are propagated from stem cuttings, using young non-flowering side shoots, again about 8cm (3in) long. Cut the bases immediately below a leaf joint or node and strip off the lower leaves. Then

▼ *Phlox maculata* Omega and *Papaver orientale* (bottom) can be **propagated** successfully from root cuttings taken during their dormant period.

treat as for basal cuttings. Often, these cuttings can be rooted in a garden frame, especially if taken in summer.

Some perennials can be propagated from root cuttings. In the dormant period some young roots are removed from the parent plant which will either have to be lifted, or have soil scraped away to expose roots. Some perennials have very thin roots, such as phlox; others such as *Papaver orientale*, or oriental poppy, have thick roots. Cut the roots into 5cm (2in) long sections. Thick roots should have a slanting cut made at the base and a flat cut at the top, so that you insert them the right way up (the top of the cutting is the part that was nearest to the crown of the plant).

Insert root cuttings in cutting compost. Thick roots are inserted vertically, with the tops just below compost level. Thin roots are liad on the surface of compost and then covered with a 12mm (½in) layer of compost, which is then lightly firmed. Water them in, then place in a greenhouse or garden frame to root. Top growth will be produced first; roots will follow later.

Seeds Seeds of various perennials can be bought from a good seedsman – both species and hybrids. You can also collect your own seeds but only from species, because seeds of hybrid plants will not come true to type.

Reasonably large seeds from hardy perennials can, if desired, be sown in a finely prepared seed bed in the open ground. However, you have more control over them if they are sown in seed trays in a greenhouse or garden frame.

Use a good-quality soil-based seed compost and make sure that the surface is level, smooth and moderately firm. Sow the seeds thinly and evenly on the surface, and then cover by sifting a layer of compost over them, the depth equalling twice the diameter of the seeds. Very fine dust-like seeds must not be covered, but should be lightly pressed into the surface with a flat piece of wood.

When the seedlings are large enough to handle easily they should be lifted carefully and potted individually into small pots – 8cm (3in) in diameter – using a good soil-based potting compost.

A

ACANTHUS
(Bear's breech)

These handsome perennials are grown for their attractive foliage and spikes of tubular flowers. Some species have spiny leaves (the name is derived from the Greek *acanthos,* meaning a spine). The plants are distinctive enough to be planted alone, but they also combine superbly with most kinds of flowering and foliage shrubs, including shrub roses.

HOW TO GROW
The best results come from fertile, well-drained soil and sun or partial shade. Plant in autumn or spring.

PROPAGATION
Divide in autumn or spring; plant root cuttings in late winter.

POPULAR SPECIES
A. mollis (S. Europe to Turkey). White or purple-flushed flowers in summer; large, deeply lobed leaves. 1–1.2m (3–4ft). *A. m. latifolius* is taller.
A. spinosus (Italy to Greece). Flowers are white, bracts are green and sometimes flushed with purple, summer; spiny, lobed, deep green leaves. 1–1.2m (3–4ft).

▲ *Achillea filipendulina*

▲ *Achillea ptarmica*

▼ *Achillea millefolium*

▼ *Acanthus mollis*

Aconitum carmichaelii 'Arendsii'

ACHILLEA

Noted for their very long flowering period in summer, the achilleas are easily grown border plants with blooms which are suitable for cutting. They look as good in modern borders as in cottage gardens.

HOW TO GROW

Achilleas need well-drained soil and plenty of sun. Plant in autumn or spring.

PROPAGATION

Divide in autumn or spring; plant basal cuttings in spring.

POPULAR SPECIES

A. filipendulina (Caucasus). Flat heads of bright yellow flowers in summer. 1–1.2m (3–4ft). Good varieties are 'Gold Plate' and 'Coronation Gold'.

A. millefolium (Europe, W. Asia). This is a lawn weed known as yarrow, but there is an excellent variety with flat heads of cerise-red flowers called 'Cerise Queen' which flowers in summer. 45cm (1½ft).

A. ptarmica (Europe to Siberia). Usually grown is the variety 'The Pearl' with double, button-like white flowers, which bloom in summer. 45cm (1½ft).

ACONITUM
(Monkshood)

These plants are widely grown in mixed borders where they produce spikes of hooded flowers in summer. All parts of the plants are poisonous so are best avoided if you have young children in the family. The deeply lobed leaves are attractive.

HOW TO GROW
They need moist soil in a sunny or partially shaded spot. Plant in autumn or spring.

PROPAGATION
Divide in autumn or spring.

POPULAR SPECIES
A. × *cammarum (A. bicolor).* A hybrid plant of which 'Blue Sceptre' and 'Bressingham Spire' are particularly recommended, with deep blue flowers in summer. 1m (3ft).
A. carmichaelii 'Arendsii'. Blue flowers in late summer and autumn. 1.2m (4ft).

ADIANTUM
(Maidenhair fern)

Most of the maidenhair ferns are from the tropics but there are two hardy species that will thrive outdoors in semi-shade, such as in a woodland garden, shrub border or on the shady side of a rock garden.

HOW TO GROW
The hardy species need a moist but well-drained soil in dappled shade. Ideally they should be planted in the spring when they can establish themselves best.

PROPAGATION
Lift and divide clumps in the spring.

▼ *Adiantum pedatum*

POPULAR SPECIES
A. pedatum (N. America, Asia). Tufted habit, forming a rosette of very deeply cut bright green fronds, deciduous. Height 15–45cm (6–18in).
A. venustum (Himalaya). This species spreads by rhizomes; the bright green fronds are triangular and up to 30cm (12in) long, carried on purple-black stalks. Height up to 30cm (12in).

▲ *Adonis amurensis*

ADONIS

Named for the Greek god of plants, adonis has deeply cut ferny leaves and buttercup-like flowers which create a charming display when planted in bold groups around shrubs or in light woodland conditions.

HOW TO GROW
Grow in well-drained soil in a sunny spot. Plant in late summer or autumn.

PROPAGATION
Lift and divide clumps either at planting time or after flowering. Sow seeds as soon as they are ripe, when they generally germinate with a high rate of success.

POPULAR SPECIES
A. amurensis (China, Japan). Yellow buttercup-like flowers are produced in late

winter and spring, set against the ferny foliage. Height up to 30cm (12in). There are several Japanese varieties, but perhaps the best-known is 'Fukujukai' with large golden-yellow flowers. The variety 'Pleniflora' has double flowers.

A. vernalis (Europe). This has bright yellow flowers in spring. 10–40cm (4–15in).

AGAPANTHUS
(African lily)

These are clump-forming evergreen or deciduous perennials with bold strap-shaped leaves and rounded heads of blue or white, tubular, lily-like flowers in summer or autumn. They are excellent plants for growing in ornamental containers and look superb grouped among shrubs.

HOW TO GROW

Deciduous species are reasonably hardy and withstand moderate frosts if grown in sheltered sunny spots with well-drained soil; the evergreens need frost protection but can be grown outside in very mild areas. Or grow them in tubs and move them under glass for the winter. Plant or pot on in the spring.

PROPAGATION

Divide clumps in the spring.

POPULAR SPECIES

A. campanulatus (South Africa). Deciduous,

▲ *Agapanthus* 'Headbourne Hybrid'

blue or white flowers in late summer. 1m (3ft). The 'Headbourne Hybrids' derive from this species and are highly recommended; many shades of blue and also white.

A. praecox (South Africa). Evergreen, with blue flowers in summer (variety 'Albus' has white flowers). 60–75cm (2–2½ft).

AJUGA
(Bugle)

These ground-cover plants form spreading, prostrate mats. Short spikes of generally blue flowers appear in the spring and the foliage is generally evergreen. They are easy and quite vigorous plants,

▼ *Ajuga reptans*

▼ *Agapanthus praecox* 'Albus'

ideal for clothing the ground around shrubs, roses and so on.

HOW TO GROW

They thrive in any ordinary soil in sun or shade. Plant in autumn or spring.

PROPAGATION

Lift and divide in spring or after flowering.

POPULAR SPECIES

A. pyramidalis (Europe). Pale violet-blue flowers in spring or summer; spikes up to 30cm (12in) high.
A. reptans (Europe to S.W. Asia). Generally varieties are grown, such as 'Alba', white flowers; 'Atropurpurea', red-purple foliage; 'Burgundy Glow', wine-red leaves; 'Multicolor' ('Rainbow'), leaves in various colours; and 'Variegata', leaves splashed grey-green and white.

△ *Alchemilla mollis*

ALCHEMILLA
(Lady's mantle)

These are herbaceous, low-growing, tufted perennials with attractive, lobed, rounded leaves and clouds of yellow-green flowers in summer. They are very popular for ground cover in shrub or mixed borders, at the edge of woodland, etc. These plants are also loved by flower arrangers because of their unusual flower colour.

HOW TO GROW

Grow in any ordinary garden soil in a sunny or shady position. Plant in autumn or spring.

PROPAGATION

Lift and divide clumps at planting time. Also grow from seeds sown in the spring.

POPULAR SPECIES

A. mollis (Carpathians to Turkey). This is the species most usually grown; it is a robust, vigorous plant with light green, soft, hairy leaves and lime-green flowers over a long period in summer. 30–45cm (1–1½ft).

ALSTROEMERIA
(Peruvian lily)

These tuberous-rooted herbaceous perennials have grassy foliage and colourful lily-like flowers in the summer or autumn. They are generally grown in herbaceous borders but are ideal for mixed borders because they make lovely companions for shrubs, especially coloured-foliage kinds.

HOW TO GROW

Grow in well-drained soil in a sunny, sheltered position. Plant in spring.

PROPAGATION

Lift and divide congested clumps in the spring.

POPULAR SPECIES

A. aurantiaca (Chile). This is the best-known species, with bright orange flowers in late summer and autumn. 1m (3ft). Several varieties, such as the golden-yellow 'Aurea' and 'Lutea', the latter with bright red markings, and the rich orange 'Dover Orange'.
A. ligtu (Chile). Flowers in shades of pale red to pink and white; summer, autumn. 60cm (2ft) or more. This species is represented in cultivation by the famous 'Ligtu Hybrids' which are slightly taller than the species. There are named varieties and the blooms come in colours which range from pink to orange-red.

Alstroemeria 'Ligtu Hybrids'

Althaea ficifolia

ALTHAEA
(Hollyhock)

These old-fashioned plants with tall spikes of rosette-like flowers in summer are traditionally grown in cottage gardens but do not look out of place in modern herbaceous or mixed borders.

HOW TO GROW

Grow in any ordinary well-drained soil; the richer the soil the taller the plants. Choose a position in full sun. Plant in spring.

PROPAGATION

Raise from seeds sown in early summer where the plants are to flower.

POPULAR SPECIES

A. ficifolia (Siberia). Short-lived perennial with deeply lobed leaves and yellow, orange or white, sometimes double, flowers. 2m (6ft) or more.

A. rosea (China). Woody-stemmed perennial with pink or red flowers, often fully double. Several varieties a wider colour range include 'Chater's Double'. 3m (10ft) or more.

ANAPHALIS
(Pearly everlasting)

These are herbaceous clump-forming perennials with narrow, often grey or white downy leaves, and clusters of generally white, papery flower heads. The flowers can be dried for use in winter arrangements. They are generally grown in herbaceous or mixed borders.

HOW TO GROW

Anaphalis is suited to any ordinary soil, provided drainage is good, and a sunny position. Plant in autumn or spring.

PROPAGATION

Lift and divide the clumps at planting time.

▲ *Anaphalis triplinervis*

POPULAR SPECIES

A. cinnamomea (A. yedoensis) (India, Burma). Leaves white-felted below; flowers produced in late summer. 75cm (2½ft).
A. triplinervis (Himalaya). Leaves grey-felted beneath, cotton-like above; flowers late summer. 30–45cm (1–1½ft). Variety 'Summer Snow' is a dwarf form of the species and has whiter flowers.

ANCHUSA
(Alkanet)

These tufted perennials have tubular bright blue flowers in spring or summer. Grow them in herbaceous or mixed borders where they are excellent for combining with yellow-flowered perennials. The low-growing species are suitable for rock gardens.

▼ *Anchusa azurea*

HOW TO GROW

Grow in any ordinary well-drained soil, preferably enriched with garden compost or well-rotted manure. Choose a sunny spot. Plant in autumn or spring.

PROPAGATION

Lift and divide at planting time; plant root cuttings in winter.

POPULAR SPECIES

A. angustissima (E. Europe). Purple-blue flowers in early summer. 22–30cm (9–12in).
A. azurea (A. italica) (Caucasus). Blue to purple-blue flowers in early summer. 90–150cm (3–5ft). There are several good varieties of this species, such as 'Loddon Royalist', gentian-blue, 90cm (3ft); and 'Opal', sky-blue, 1–2m (3–6ft).

ANEMONE
(Windflower)

This is a large genus and very variable in habit, but the perennials usually grown are hybrids which flower in late summer or autumn, bringing invaluable colour at that time of year. The flowers of some species are like large buttercups and bloom over a very long period.

HOW TO GROW

Grow in any ordinary well-drained soil in full sun or partial shade. This plant grows especially well on chalky soils. Plant in autumn or spring.

PROPAGATION

Lift and divide congested clumps at planting time. They are best left undisturbed for as long as possible.

POPULAR SPECIES

A. × hybrida (A. japonica, A. elegans). Popularly called Japanese anemone; a hybrid plant of which there are numerous varieties, including 'Bressingham Glow', pink-red flowers; 'Queen Charlotte', pink; 'September Charm', soft pink; and 'White Giant', pure white. 45–60cm (1–1½ft).

ANTHEMIS
(Chamomile)

These are attractive herbaceous perennials usually with feathery foliage and a long season of daisy-like flowers. They make excellent plants for herbaceous or mixed borders and the flowers are suitable for cutting.

HOW TO GROW

Any well-drained soil is suitable but plenty of sun is needed. Suitable for hot dry spots. Plant in autumn or spring.

PROPAGATION

Lift and divide established clumps at planting time, or take basal cuttings in the spring and root in a cold frame.

▲ *Anthemis cupaniana*

▼ *Anthemis tinctoria* 'E. C. Buxton'

POPULAR SPECIES

A. cupaniana (Italy). A low mat- or cushion-forming plant with fern-like silver-grey foliage and white flowers in summer and autumn. 15cm (6in) or more. Ideal for the front of a border.

A. tinctoria (Europe). Clump-forming, with fern-like foliage and yellow flowers in summer. 60–90cm (2–3ft). Generally varieties are grown, such as 'E.C. Buxton', lemon-yellow; 'Grallagh Gold', deep yellow; and 'Wargrave', pale creamy-yellow.

AQUILEGIA
(Columbine)

These tufted, clump-forming herbaceous plants are traditionally planted in cottage gardens. They look equally good, though, in modern mixed, herbaceous or shrub borders. The funnel-shaped flowers, which have long spurs at the back, are offset by the compound foliage.

HOW TO GROW

Grow in well-drained soil enriched with humus, so dig in garden compost or well-rotted manure before planting. Aquilegias thrive in full sun or partial shade. Plant in autumn or spring.

PROPAGATION

Lift and divide established clumps in the spring just as growth is commencing. Or raise from seeds, ideally sown as soon as ripe. Seeds of hybrids can also be bought from seedsmen.

POPULAR SPECIES

A. caerulea (Rocky Mountains, USA). This species produces long-spurred blue and white flowers in late spring and summer. 30–60cm (1–2ft).

A. canadensis (USA). The colour of the flowers is a combination of yellow or red, and lemon-yellow, and the spurs are about 2cm (1in) long; late spring to summer. 30cm (12in) or more.

A. longissima (Texas to Mexico). Deeply lobed leaflets with a blue-white sheen; pale yellow flowers with 10–15cm (4–6in) long

▲ *Aquilegia × bybrida*　　　　　　▼ *Artemisia stellerana*

spurs; summer to autumn. 60–90cm (2–3ft).
A. vulgaris (Europe). The species itself,
with flowers in shades of purple or red, is
not usually grown, but rather the various
named strains or varieties. Well-known
varieties are the 'McKana Hybrids'; they have
very long spurs and flower in a wide range of
colours; 90cm (3ft).

ARTEMISIA

The herbaceous perennial species often
have attractive grey or white foliage and
make marvellous companions for shrubs,
particularly purple-leaved kinds. They are
very attractive in cottage gardens.

▲ *Arum creticum*

HOW TO GROW

Artemisias need well-drained soil in full sun, and are ideal for hot dry positions. Plant in autumn or spring.

PROPAGATION

Lift and divide, or take basal cuttings and plant in spring.

POPULAR SPECIES

A. lactiflora (China, India). Deeply cut fern-like foliage and cream plume-like flower heads in late summer. It is the only species grown for flowers alone. 1.8m (6ft).
A. ludoviciana (USA, Mexico). Vigorous; leaves white-felted below, grey-white above; white flowers in summer. 1.2m (4ft).

A. stellerana (N.E. Asia, N. Europe, USA). Fine feathery foliage, silvery grey. One of the finest artemisias and popularly called dusty miller. 30–60cm (1–2ft).

ARUM

Tuberous-rooted perennials with attractive arrow-like leaves, the flowers consist of a spathe and spadix (rather sail-like in shape). They are unusual but easily grown subjects for the edge of a shrub border or woodland garden.

HOW TO GROW

Generally hardy, these plants thrive in any

▲ *Arum italicum* 'Pictum'

leaves and pale yellow to white spathes, with a gold spadix; spring. Suited to gardens in mild areas only. 40cm (just more than 1ft). *A. italicum* (Mediterranean, S. to Sardinia and Cyprus, W. Europe). Variable habit, with narrow to broad leaves, sometimes veined yellow or white; spathe palest yellow, late spring. 30–60cm (1–2ft). *A. i.* 'Pictum' has narrow, dark green leaves which are boldly veined with white. *A. i.* 'Marmoratum' has broader leaves dappled with grey.

soil which is moisture-retentive and high in humus. They are suitable for sun or partial shade. Plant in late summer to autumn.

PROPAGATION

Detach offsets when the plants are dormant.

POPULAR SPECIES

A. creticum (Crete, S. Greece). Plain green

ARUNCUS
(Goat's beard)

This is a large, distinctive, herbaceous perennial which can be grown either alone as a specimen plant – say in a lawn – or combined with shrubs in a shrub border. It associates particularly well with purple-leaved shrubs and looks good, too, with shrub roses.

HOW TO GROW

This plant needs a moist soil in partial shade or sun. Plant in autumn or spring.

▽ *Aruncus dioicus*

PROPAGATION

Lift and divide established clumps in autumn or spring.

POPULAR SPECIES

A. dioicus (A. sylvester, A. vulgaris, Spiraea aruncus) (N. Hemisphere). This is the only species grown. It is a vigorous, clump-forming plant with large compound leaves and huge plumes of creamy-white flowers in the summer. 2m (6ft). The variety 'Kneiffi' is smaller than the species, about 1m (3ft) high, and better suited to small gardens.

ASPHODELINE
(Asphodel)

These are unusual-looking herbaceous plants but with a distinctive character. They form tufts or clumps of upright stems which bear grassy foliage and heads of starry flowers with long curled stamens. They can be grown in a herbaceous border, but look best when associated with shrubs.

HOW TO GROW

Asphodels need well-drained soil in a sunny, sheltered position. Plant them in the autumn or spring.

PROPAGATION

Lift and divide clumps in the spring, or sow seeds in spring.

POPULAR SPECIES

A. liburnica (S.E. Europe). A smaller and more slender version of *A. lutea,* described below. Flowers a little paler and bloom later.
A. lutea (Asphodelus luteus) (S.E. Europe, Algeria, Tunisia, Israel). Known as the yellow asphodel, this is the best-known species, with yellow flowers in spring and summer; foliage grey-green. Stiff, upright stems up to 90cm (3ft).

ASPLENIUM
(Spleenwort)

A large group of ferns, most of which are tender, but there are some hardy species suitable for the garden. These are ideal for rock gardens or dry-stone walls and they have a tufted habit of growth.

HOW TO GROW

Spleenworts need a well-drained gritty soil with peat or leaf-mould added; grow in sun or partial shade. Plant in spring.

PROPAGATION

Divide in spring.

POPULAR SPECIES

A. adiantum-nigrum (N. Hemisphere, South Africa). This is the black spleenwort, so-called because it has black stalks. The fronds are triangular in shape and up to 50cm (1ft 8in) long.
A. trichomanes (N. and S. temperate zones, tropical mountains). Called the maidenhair spleenwort it has pinnate (compound) fronds up to 20cm (8in) long; the stalks are a dark red-brown.

▽ *Asphodeline lutea*

ASTER
(Michaelmas daisy)

Michaelmas daisies represent the very essence of autumn and should be grown in every garden, either in herbaceous beds or borders or, perhaps even better, in a shrub border, around shrubs which have autumn leaf tints and/or berries. They are herbaceous in habit and very easily grown – indeed they spread quite vigorously and regularly need lifting and dividing. The daisy-like flowers are produced from late summer to mid-autumn.

▲ Aster novae-angliae 'Harrington's Pink'

▼ Aster novi-belgii

HOW TO GROW

Grow in any ordinary soil that does not dry out excessively, and ideally in full sun, although good results are possible in partial shade. The tall varieties generally need supports, because they are inclined to flop over in wet and windy weather. Insert twiggy sticks around the clumps just as growth is starting. The height of these sticks should be slightly below the ultimate height of the plant. Plant in autumn or spring.

PROPAGATION

Lift and divide in spring. This can be done annually if desired, but at least every other year to keep the plants young and vigorous.

POPULAR SPECIES

A. acris (A. sedifolius) (S. and E. Europe). Large, bright blue, daisy-like flowers are produced in late summer. One of the first Michaelmas daisies to come into flower. 60–90cm (2–3ft).

A. amellus (C. and S. Europe). Usually varieties of this are grown, such as the very well-known 'King George', with violet-blue flowers in late summer. 60cm (2ft).

A. × frikartii. Large, bright, glossy purple-blue flowers with yellow centres in summer and autumn. 80cm (2½ft).

A. novae-angliae (E. USA). Generally varieties of this are grown, such as 'Harrington's Pink', clear pink; and 'Lye End Beauty', phlox-purple. Flowers are produced in autumn. Up to 1.5m (5ft).

A. novi-belgii (E. USA). The most popular Michaelmas daisy. There are scores of varieties; some are dwarf plants 30-45cm (1–1½ft) high, others are tall, up to 1.2 or 1.5m (4 or 5ft) in height. They are autumn flowering and colours include all shades of blue, purple, red, pink and white.

ASTILBE

These beautiful herbaceous perennials have attractive pinnate leaves and feathery plumes of flowers in the summer. The plants form substantial clumps and look particularly lovely when planted beside a pool or among shrubs.

HOW TO GROW

A moisture-retentive soil is necessary, in sun or shade. Plant in autumn or spring.

PROPAGATION

Lift and divide established clumps in the autumn or spring.

POPULAR SPECIES

A. × *arendsii.* This is a hybrid group containing lots of named varieties: e.g. 'Bressingham Beauty', pink; 'Deutschland', white; 'Fanal', deep red; 'Rhineland', pink. 60–90cm (2–3ft).

▲ *Astrantia major*

▲ *Astilbe* × *arendsii*

A. chinensis 'Pumila' (China). Mauve-pink flowers, spreads widely. 30cm (12in).

ASTRANTIA
(Masterwort)

Herbaceous plants with attractive lobed or compound leaves, astrantias have rounded flower heads surrounded by a ruff of papery bracts, which are carried on upright stems. They are often grown in woodland gardens but they are also a good choice for shrub borders.

HOW TO GROW

Grow in shade or sun, in moisture-retentive soil (but not prone to waterlogging), rich in

▲ *Astrantia maxima*

humus such as peat or leaf-mould. Plant in autumn or spring.

PROPAGATION

Lift and divide clumps at planting time.

POPULAR SPECIES

A. carniolica (Austria, Italy, Yugoslavia). White or pink-flushed flowers in summer; *A.c.* 'Rubra' has red-purple flower heads. 30cm (12in) or more.
A. major (C. and E. Europe). Green-white flowers, sometimes tinted pink or purple, summer. *A.m.* 'Rubra' has plum-red flowers and *A.m.* 'Sunningdale Variegated' has yellow variegated foliage. 60–90cm (2–3ft).
A. maxima (Caucasus, Turkey). Rose-pink in summer. 60cm (2ft).

B

BERGENIA
(Pig-squeak)

These evergreen spring-flowering perennials grow from thick fleshy rhizomes and produce tufts of large, rounded to paddle-shaped, leathery leaves and large trusses of somewhat bell-shaped flowers.

The bergenias are among the most useful of the evergreen perennials. The foliage is quite dramatic (especially when the plants are set in bold groups) and associates well with all kinds of shrubs and with perennials which have grassy or woolly foliage. They are an excellent choice for patio plants because they contrast superbly with paving and architecture. They make good dense ground cover, too, particularly between shrubs.

HOW TO GROW

Grow in humus-rich soil (add peat or leaf-mould) in partial shade, preferably sheltered from strong winds to avoid leaf damage. Plant in autumn or spring.

PROPAGATION

Lift and divide established clumps at planting time. Cut some rhizomes into 5cm (2in) long sections in winter and root these in a heated propagator.

POPULAR SPECIES

B. ciliata (W. Himalaya). White flowers, becoming flushed with red, spring. Liable to frost damage. 30–45cm (1–1½ft).
B. cordifolia (Siberia). Pale to deep rose-pink flowers, spring. *B.c.* 'Purpurea' has leaves flushed with purple, and rose-magenta flowers. 30cm (12in).
B. crassifolia (Siberia). Rose-purple flowers, spring. 30cm (12in).
B. hybrids (German origin). 'Abendglut' ('Evening Glow'), deep purple; 'Morgenrote' ('Morning Red'), red-purple; 'Silberlicht' ('Silver Light'), white, turning slightly pink with age. All flower in spring. 30–45cm (1–1½ft) high.

B. purpurascens (B.delavayi) (Himalya, N. Burma, W. China). Leaves flushed with red; flowers bright pink to deep purple-red in spring. 40cm (1ft 4in). *B.p.* 'Ballawley' (*B.p.* Delbees) is very large and vigorous, with magenta flowers.
B. smithii. A hybrid with red or purple-edged leaves; deep pink flowers, spring. 30cm (12in). Varieties include 'Bressingham Bountiful', bright pink; 'Margery Fish', glowing pink; 'Pugsley's Purple', purple; 'Sunningdale', deep purple.

▲ *Bergenia purpurascens*

▼ *Bergenia purpurascens* 'Ballawley'

C

CALAMINTHA
(Calamint)

These aromatic perennials were originally used instead of the closely related savory or satureja, to which they are closely related. The oval leaves have a powerful scent and in summer spikes of small,

CAMPANULA
(Bellflower)

Herbaceous perennials, some with bell-shaped flowers in summer, generally in shades of blue, but also purple and white. They are excellent, easily grown border plants, and can be grown with other perennials in a herbaceous border, or with shrubs in a mixed border. They associate particularly well with old and modern shrub

▲ *Calamintha nepeta*

▲ *Campanula carpatica*

tubular, lipped flowers are produced. This is a charming plant for a cottage garden, or for a mixed border in modern gardens.

H O W T O G R O W
Calamintha needs a very well-drained soil in full sun. Plant calamintha in the autumn or in the spring.

P R O P A G A T I O N
Lift and divide established clumps in spring.

P O P U L A R S P E C I E S
C. nepeta (C. nepetoides, Satureja calamintha) (mountains of S. and S. C. Europe). This is a strongly aromatic upright perennial which spreads by a long, creeping rhizome. It has grey, hairy stems, oval, toothed leaves and grey and lilac or white flowers in late summer and autumn. 40–80cm (1ft 4in–2ft 8in) high.

roses. Because most bellflowers produce their flowers in spikes, good contrast in shape is achieved if they are planted with flat-headed perennials, such as some of the species of achilleas.

H O W T O G R O W
Bellflowers need well-drained soil but will grow in any type, in full sun or partial shade. Plant in autumn or spring.

P R O P A G A T I O N
Lift and divide established clumps at planting time. Plant basal cuttings in spring.

P O P U L A R S P E C I E S
C. carpatica (Carpathian Mountains). A dwarf clump-forming perennial suitable for the front of the border. The blue flowers are an open bell shape, produced in summer. 20–50cm (8–20in). Good varieties include

Campanula lactiflora 'Prichard's'

Catananche caerulea

'Alba', with white flowers, and 'Turbinata' with blue flowers.

C. lactiflora (Caucasus). Clump-forming perennial with blue, open funnel-shaped flowers in summer and autumn. 1.5m (5ft). Good varieties are 'Alba', white; 'Loddon Anna', lilac-pink, and 'Pritchard's', with violet-blue flowers.

C. latifolia (Europe). Clump-forming perennial with blue to violet-blue flowers in summer. 1.5m (5ft). Varieties include 'Alba', white; 'Brantwood', rich violet-purple; 'Macrantha', purple-blue.

C. persicifolia (Europe, Asia). Peach-leaved bellflower with blue flowers in summer and early autumn. 90cm (3ft). Several varieties in various shades of blue or white.

CATANANCHE
(Cupid's Dart)

The name comes from the Greek *katanangke*, meaning a strong incentive – the plant was formerly used in love potions. This is a tufted perennial with narrow lower leaves and wiry stems that bear daisy-like flowers in summer. It is a charming little plant for cottage gardens or mixed borders; plant it near the front.

HOW TO GROW
Grow in any well-drained soil in a sunny position. Plant in spring or autumn.

PROPAGATION
Plant root cuttings in late winter or sow seed in spring.

POPULAR SPECIES
C. caerulea (Portugal to Italy). Popularly called the blue cupidone, this is the only species grown. It has lavender-blue flowers in the summer. *C.c.* 'Major' has larger and brighter flowers. 50–80cm (1ft 8in–2½ft).

CENTAUREA

These perennials are variable in habit of growth. They have daisy-like flowers and are invaluable for providing colour in mixed or herbaceous borders during the summer. Many species have very pretty silvery leaves. The flowers are also suitable for cutting and are an excellent choice for cottage or cottage-style gardens.

HOW TO GROW
Centaureas will grow in any well-drained soil provided it is reasonably fertile. A position in

upper surface, and silvery underneath. 45–100cm(1½–3ft).

C. macrocephala(Caucasus). Very large, deep yellow, powder-puff-like flowers in summer. 90cm (3ft).

C. montana (mountains of Europe). Deep purple-blue flowers, late spring to summer. Ideal for front of border. Up to 60cm (2ft) tall. White and pink forms are available.

▲ *Centaurea montana*

▼ *Centaurea macrocephala*

full sun is essential. Plant in autumn or spring.

PROPAGATION
Lift and divide established clumps in the autumn or spring.

POPULAR SPECIES
C. dealbata (Caucasus). Lilac-pink flowers in summer. The leaves are grey-green on the

CENTRANTHUS
(Valerian)

A popular and very easily grown perennial, this is ideal for hot dry situations such as sunny banks. It often grows in old walls. Also use it at the front of herbaceous or mixed borders, and in cottage gardens, where it is traditionally grown.

HOW TO GROW
Grow in any well-drained soil in a sunny position. Plant in spring or autumn.

PROPAGATION
Sow seeds when ripe or in the spring. Plant basal cuttings in late spring.

POPULAR SPECIES
C. ruber (C. and S. Europe, N. Africa, Turkey). This is the only species grown. It has grey-green foliage and heads of small tubular red, pink or white flowers in summer and autumn. It has an exceptionally long flowering period. The form C.r. 'Albus' bears white flowers. Up to 90cm (3ft) tall.

▼ *Centranthus ruber*

CHELONE
(Turtle-head)

This is the Greek word for tortoise and refers to the flowers, which fancifully resemble a reptilian head. It is a clump-forming plant which bears spikes of hooded tubular flowers in summer or autumn. It is highly recommended for inclusion in herbaceous and mixed borders.

HOW TO GROW

Chelone needs a moisture-retentive, humus-rich soil (add garden compost, peat or leaf-mould before planting). Choose a position either in full sun or in partial shade. Plant in autumn or spring.

PROPAGATION

Lift and divide established clumps at planting time. Sow seeds in spring.

POPULAR SPECIES

C. obliqua (S.E. USA). Rose-purple flowers with a yellow 'beard' appear in late summer and autumn. Height up to 1m (3ft).

▲ *Chelone obliqua*

▼ Flowers of *Chelone obliqua*

CHRYSANTHEMUM

Hardy chrysanthemums for the herbaceous or mixed border include the popular Shasta daisies and the early-flowering florists' chrysanthemums. The latter herald the autumn and should be grown in every garden to provide welcome colour in that season, along with Michaelmas daisies and shrubs with autmn leaf colour and/or berries. All chrysanthemums are highly suitable for cutting and consequently are popular with flower arrangers.

HOW TO GROW

All chrysanthemums need well-drained soil but will grow in any type. However, it needs to be reasonably fertile so add garden compost or well-rotted manure before planting. A position in full sun is essential. Plant in the spring, preferably, or in autumn if the soil is light and very well drained.

PROPAGATION

Lift and divide established clumps of Shasta daisies and early-flowering chrysanthemums at planting time. The early-flowering chrysanthemums can also be propagated from basal cuttings taken in spring and rooted under glass.

POPULAR SPECIES

Chrysanthemum maximum (Leucanthemum maximum) (Pyrenees). This is the well-loved Shasta daisy, an extremely easy-to-grow and long-flowering perennial with white daisy-like flowers in

▲ *Chrysanthemum* 'Tracey Waller'

summer, continuing into the autumn. Several varieties are available with double or anemone-centred blooms – 'Everest', 'Mayfield Giant' and 'Wirral Supreme' are well-tried popular varieties. 60–90cm (2–3ft). *Early-flowering chrysanthemums* (florists' chrysanthemums) are a race of hybrid varieties derived from *C. vestitum (C. morifolium)*, *C. indicum* and probably other species. They originated in China before 500 BC, then were further developed by the Japanese from about AD 800 onwards. Chinese varieties reached Britain via France in 1795 and Japanese varieties arrived direct in 1861. Since then numerous varieties have been bred in the western world.

The early-flowering chrysanthemums grow to about 1–1.2m (3–4ft) in height and have large flowers. The blooms are ball-shaped and the petals either curve tightly towards the centre, or curve outwards and downwards. These are undoubtedly the best of the outdoor chrysanthemums for cutting and last for many weeks in water. There is a very wide range of colours including shades of red, pink, yellow, orange and white.

Also well worth growing in borders are the garden spray chrysanthemums, the blooms of which make excellent cut flowers. As the name suggests, the flowers are produced in sprays, in an equally wide range of colours, during the autumn. The flowers are double. Height 1–1.2m (3–4ft).

The pompon chrysanthemums are best mass planted for a really eye-catching

▲ *Chrysanthemum maximum*

▲ *Chrysanthemum* 'Marjorie Boden'

▼ *Chrysanthemum* 'Honeyball'

display. They are dwarf, bushy plants, varying from 45 to 60cm (1½–2ft) in height, and smother themselves with small blooms between late summer and mid-autumn. The 5cm (2in) wide blooms are pompon-like and come in a wide range of colours. They are also suitable for cutting.

CIMICIFUGA
(Bugbane)

One of the species was formerly used as an insect repellent, hence the common name. The bugbanes are herbaceous perennials with fluffy wand-like spikes of flowers in summer. They are excellent plants for creating variations in shape and texture in herbaceous or mixed borders.

▲ *Cimicifuga simplex*

HOW TO GROW
Grow cimicifuga in a humus-rich soil. Preferably grow in partial shade, although full sun is tolerated if the soil is moist. Plant in autumn or spring.

PROPAGATION
Lift and divide established clumps in the autumn or spring.

POPULAR SPECIES
C. racemosa (E. USA). Known as black snakeroot, this species bears white plume-like flowers about 1 cm (½in) or more wide in summer. 1.5–2.4m (5–8ft).
C. simplex (N. temperate zones). Dense, pure white, arching, bottle-brush-like flowers, autumn. 1.2m (4ft).

CLEMATIS

Most clematis are climbers but there are several herbaceous kinds which make low bushy plants and flower in the summer or autumn. They are excellent border plants – for either mixed or herbaceous borders – and are a good choice for informal cottage gardens.

▲ *Clematis integrifolia* 'Hendersonii'

HOW TO GROW
Grow in humus-rich soil which is moisture retentive but well drained, ideally with the root area in shade and the top of the plant in sun. Dwarf perennials can provide the root-shade. Plant in autumn or spring.

PROPAGATION
Take basal cuttings in the spring and root under glass.

POPULAR SPECIES
C. heracleifolia (China). This has attractive

compound foliage against which the fragrant, blue, autumn flowers show up beautifully. 60–90cm (2–3ft).

C. integrifolia (C. and S.E. Europe to C. Asia). Nodding, usually solitary, violet-blue flowers in summer. 'Hendersonii' is a variety with larger and deeper blue flowers. 90–120cm (3–4ft).

△ *Convallaria majalis*

CONVALLARIA
(Lily-of-the-valley)

This popular dwarf herbaceous plant, which spreads by rhizomes, forms dense colonies that make good ground cover between shrubs and other plants. The plant is valued for its sweetly and strongly fragrant flowers.

HOW TO GROW
Grow in any humus-rich soil in partial shade. Plant after flowering or in autumn.

PROPAGATION
Divide at planting time.

POPULAR SPECIES
C. majalis (N. temperate zone). This is the only species. It has large, deep green, elliptic leaves and, in the spring, nodding, rounded, bell-shaped, waxy, white flowers which give off a powerful perfume. Suitable for cutting. Varieties include 'Major' and 'Fortin's Giant' with larger flowers; 'Prolificans' with double flowers; and the pale pink 'Rosea'. 15–20cm (6–8in).

COREOPSIS

These bright, colourful daisy-like perennials should be grown in every herbaceous or mixed border. The flowers are suitable for cutting.

HOW TO GROW
Grow in a well-drained, humus-rich soil in a sunny site. Plant in spring or autumn.

PROPAGATION
Lift and divide established clumps at planting time, or plant basal cuttings in the spring.

POPULAR SPECIES
C. auriculata (S.E. USA). 5cm (2in) flower heads, yellow, maroon at base, in summer. 75cm (2½ft). *C.a. 'Superba'* is more robust with larger flower.

C. grandiflora (S.E. USA). Large, bright yellow, daisy-like flowers are produced over a long period in summer. Flowering generally continues into autumn. 45–90cm (1½–3ft).

C. verticillata (S.E. USA). Slender stems bearing fern-like foliage and bright yellow flowers in summer and autumn. Usually

▽ *Coreopsis auriculata 'Superba'*

grown is the variety 'Grandiflora' which is more robust. 60cm (2ft) or more.

Coreopsis verticillata

CORTADERIA
(Pampas grass)

Large, tufted, clump-forming grasses with arching leaves and large, feathery, plume-like flowers in late summer and autumn. Pampas grass is generally used as an isolated specimen, in a lawn, for example. But it is marvellous in association with autumn-colouring shrubs, particularly if planted near a pond or pool.

HOW TO GROW

Pampas grass flourishes in any well-drained soil in a sunny position. Ideally plant it in spring; otherwise, in early autumn. Remove

Cortaderia s. 'Sunningdale Silver'

dead leaves to encourage growth.

PROPAGATION

Lift and divide established clumps in spring or early autumn.

POPULAR SPECIES

C. richardii (C. conspicua) (New Zealand). Thick clumps of long leaves with lighter green midrib. Plumes of cream flowers in late summer; short-lived 1.5–2.75m (5–9ft).
C. selloana (C. argentea) (temperate S. America). Leaves up to 3m (10ft) long; white flowers in early autumn. Up to 3m (10ft) tall. *C.s.* 'Pumila' is a dwarf variety, 1.5m (5ft) high; *C.s.* 'Rendatleri' has rose-purple tinted flowers, 3m (10ft); and *C.s.* 'Sunningdale Silver' is a popular variety with creamy white plumes, 2m (6ft) or more.

CORYDALIS

These generally low-growing, tufted perennials have attractive fern-like foliage and tubular spurred flowers which bloom in spring or summer. They are charming little plants for the front of shrub borders or for planting in light woodland conditions.

HOW TO GROW

Corydalis needs a moisture-retentive yet

Corydalis lutea

well-drained soil in partial shade or in full sun. Plant in autumn or spring.

PROPAGATION

Divide at planting time, or sow seeds as soon as they are ripe.

POPULAR SPECIES

C. bulbosa (C. cava) (Europe). Grows from a tuber; grey-green frond-like foliage; dusky pink flowers, spring; short-lived. 10–15cm (4–6in).
C. lutea (Europe, C. and S. Alps but widely naturalized elsewhere). Dense, tufted little plant with compound leaves, giving a fern-like appearance, grey-green undersurface; golden-yellow flowers with darker tip, spring to autumn. Excellent for growing in old walls, but rather invasive in the garden proper (ideal for natural or 'wild' areas). 15–40cm (6–15in).

CRAMBE

This is the Greek name for a wild cabbage. The species grown is a massive herbaceous perennial, ideal for the back of large herbaceous or mixed borders. It also makes a good specimen plant.

HOW TO GROW

Crambe is best planted in a humus-rich soil, so add garden compost or well-rotted manure before planting. The soil should be well drained and the position sunny. Plant in autumn or spring.

PROPAGATION

Sow seeds, divide or plant root cuttings, all in spring.

POPULAR SPECIES

C. cordifolia (Caucasus). This is the only species commonly cultivated. The lower leaves are somewhat fleshy, deep green, lobed and wavy, and grow up to 1m (3ft) long. The stems are 2m (6ft) or more tall, much branched, bearing numerous small white flowers with a strong scent, creating the illusion of a giant gypsophila. The flowers are produced in summer.

▲ *Crambe cordifolia*

▼ *Crocosmia masonorum*

CROCOSMIA

These are very useful late-flowering herbaceous perennials, with grassy foliage and sprays of bright lily-like flowers. The flowering time is late summer and perhaps into early autumn.

HOW TO GROW

Grow in well-drained humus-rich soil that does not dry out, in sun or light shade. Plant in spring.

PROPAGATION

Lift and divide established clumps at planting time.

POPULAR SPECIES

All originate from South Africa.
C. × *crocosmiiflora*. Popularly called montbretia. The original orange-red hybrid has become naturalized in many parts of the world, including Britain. Recommended varieties: 'Citronella', soft lemon-yellow;

'Jackanapes', deep red and yellow; 'Solfatare', pale apricot-yellow. 60cm (2ft).
C. masonorum. This species has brilliant vermilion-orange flowers. 1m (3ft). Some excellent hybrids between this and *Curtonus paniculatus* include 'Bressingham Blaze', flame-red, and 'Emberglow', burnt orange.

D

DAHLIA

These are tuberous-rooted tender perennials which make a brilliant display in the summer and through to autumn, being stopped only by the first frosts. They are ideal for herbaceous or mixed borders, the blooms being excellent for cutting and arranging in water.

HOW TO GROW

Grow in well-drained yet moisture-retentive soil rich in humus such as garden compost or well-rotted manure. It should also be quite fertile. They must be grown in a very sunny site, protected from winds.

Plant out young plants in late spring or early summer, when all danger of frost is over. Dormant tubers can be planted in mid-spring. Tubers should be lifted in autumn and stored dry for the winter in a cool, dry frost-proof place.

▲ *Dahlia* 'Lavendale'

PROPAGATION

Take cuttings from the old tubers in spring and propagate in a heated greenhouse. Large clumps of tubers can be divided in the spring before being planted out.

POPULAR SPECIES

The dahlias commonly available are varieties originally derived from forms of *D. variabilis* (*D. coccinea, D. pinnata, D. rosea*), from the

▼ *Dahlia* 'Rose Willo'

▼ *Dahlia* 'Ruwenzori'

high plains of Mexico. These range in height from less than 30cm (12in) to 1.5m (5ft). The compound leaves are flushed with bronze or purple in some varieties. The flower heads may be single, semi-double or double in shades of white, yellow, red, orange, purple and pink, with many two-colour combinations. The varieties have been placed into well-defined groups.

DELPHINIUM

Delphiniums are among the most popular of border plants, especially the *elatum* hybrids which have very tall thick spikes of flowers in the summer, mainly in shades of blue but in other colours also.

The tall delphiniums are almost essential subjects for the back of herbaceous borders, combined with flowers of contrasting form and colour, such as flat-headed, yellow achilleas.

Some dramatic groups can also be created in mixed borders by combining delphiniums with shrubs and roses. For instance, blue delphiniums associate particularly well with purple-leaved shrubs such as varieties of *Cotinus coggygria,* or smoke bush, and *Berberis,* or barberry. There are few better companions for shrub roses, old and modern, than the tall delphiniums. Try bold groups of blue or purple varieties with shrub roses in shades of red or pink.

▼ *Delphinium*, typical garden hybrid

▼ *Delphinium*, typical garden hybrid

▲ *Delphinium*, typical garden hybrids

No cottage garden is complete without delphiniums, again, perhaps, growing them with old-fashioned roses, such as the moss and Provence roses.

HOW TO GROW

Delphiniums appreciate good growing conditions, so it is advisable, if you want the tallest, fattest spikes of flowers, to grow them in the right conditions and to prepare the soil well before planting. The site should be sunny and preferably sheltered from strong winds. Grow in fertile, moisture-retentive but well-drained soil, enriched with garden compost or well-rotted manure, especially for the hybrid delphiniums. Plant in autumn or spring – spring if the soil is not very well drained.

PROPAGATION

All can be raised from seeds sown in the spring, but seed collected from hybrids will not come true to type. Alternatively, divide clumps in the spring; or during that season take basal cuttings and root them under the protection of glass.

POPULAR SPECIES

D. × *belladonna*. Probably a cross between *D. elatum* and *D. grandiflorum* and not unlike the *elatum* hybrids, but having the branched flower heads and elegantly well-spaced flowers of *D. grandiflorum*. There are several varieties available, mainly in shades of blue, but also purple, pink and white, which flower in summer. 1–1.5m (3–5ft).

D. cardinale (California, Mexico). Short-lived tufted perennial, bearing cup-shaped scarlet flowers with yellow centres in late summer. It will flower in the first year if the seeds are sown under glass in early spring. 1m (3ft).

D. elatum (Pyrenees to Mongolia). The species itself is not usually grown, but rather the hybrids (obtained by crossing this species with *D. exaltatum* and *D. formosum)*. These have strong, tall spikes of single or double blooms in a wide range of blue, purple, pink, white and cream shades, and range in height from 1–2.4m (3–8ft). More

recently the red species *D. cardinale* and *D. nudicaule* have been used in breeding, and hybrids in shades of red have evolved.

D. grandiflorum (Siberia, China). Tufted perennial with blue to violet flowers in summer. 30–90cm (1–3ft).

D. nudicaule (California, Oregon). Tufted species with deep red, spurred flowers in late spring to summer. 25–50cm (10–20in).

DIANTHUS
(Carnations and pinks)

Many of the border carnations and the old-fashioned and modern garden pinks are delightfully scented and grown for this characteristic alone. Besides scent, they all

▼ *Delphinium nudicaule*

make a long show of colour in the summer and are ideal for edging beds and borders. The blooms are excellent for cutting, especially those of border carnations.

All are at home in herbaceous and mixed borders and look especially attractive when planted around roses of all kinds, but especially shrub roses. No cottage garden is complete without some of the old-fashioned garden pinks. Many dianthus have attractive grey-green foliage which persists all the year round, and the flowers are rounded in shape, fully double in the case of border carnations.

HOW TO GROW

All dianthus are ideal plants for alkaline soils; if the soil is too acid, lime or chalk can be added. The soil must be well drained, and a sunny position is essential for strong growth and prolific flowering. Plant in autumn or spring – the spring is best if the soil is inclined to lie wet and cold throughout the winter.

PROPAGATION

Carnations and pinks are rather short-lived and need replacing regularly with young plants, which in any case have a neater habit and flower much more freely than older plants. Propagate by planting cuttings in summer or early autumn. Pinks and carnations may also be layered in the summer.

POPULAR SPECIES

D. caryophyllus (C. Mediterranean). This is the well-known carnation. The species is not grown but rather the many hybrids which have largely been derived from it. The border carnations are hardy but often short-lived and best propagated every second year. Staking and disbudding are required for quality blooms, but for general garden display are not considered necessary. The flowers, always double, may be of one colour only (selfs); or several colours (fancies); or the petals may be edged with a contrasting colour (picotees). The blooms are produced in mid- to late summer. 60–90cm (2–3ft). There are many varieties to choose from: selection depends on personal preference

Dianthus, free-flowering modern pink

for colour, scent, etc.

D. plumarius (S.W. Europe). This is the wild pink, which is not cultivated. It is believed, though, that garden pinks are largely derived from this species, with certain characteristics from other species via hybridization. They have single or double flowers of one or more colours.

The old-fashioned pinks are well-loved garden plants. Replace with young plants every four years. They flower in summer. 20–30cm (8–12in). Some very well-known varieties are 'Dad's Favourite' (white and purple), and 'Mrs Sinkins' (white).

The modern pinks are more vigorous and generally somewhat larger in all their parts. They also flower more freely, giving a main display in summer and a lesser one in autumn. Replace with young plants every two or three years. There are many varieties, but one of the best, and highly popular, is 'Doris' (light salmon-pink).

DIASCIA

These perennials originate from South Africa and the species grown is a mat-forming plant ideal for the front of a warm border, or for planting in paving or gravel areas such as patios.

HOW TO GROW

Grow in well-drained, humus-rich soil in a sheltered, sunny site. The species described

△ *Diascia cordata*

is half-hardy and in cold areas may need protection. Young plants can be overwintered in a garden frame.

PROPAGATION

Plant cuttings in spring or late summer, and sow seeds in spring.

POPULAR SPECIES

D. cordata (Lesotho). Deep green, somewhat glossy, small leaves, making a good background for the terracotta-pink flowers that are produced in summer to early autumn. Height when in flower, up to 15cm (6in).

DICENTRA

Clump-forming herbaceous plants, invaluable for colour in the spring, and with attractive fern-like foliage. Because dicentras thrive in shade they are highly recommended for planting in bold groups in shrub borders or in a woodland garden. They do equally well in herbaceous borders or in herbaceous island beds: give them a frontal position because they are dwarf plants. Cottage gardens should not be without the favourite *Dicentra spectabilis,* or bleeding heart.

HOW TO GROW

Grow in humus-rich soil (add peat or leaf-mould before planting), in sun or shade. The soil should be moisture retentive yet well drained. Plant in autumn or spring.

PROPAGATION

Divide at planting time, or plant root cuttings in late winter in a garden frame.

POPULAR SPECIES

D. eximia (E. USA). Spreads by rhizomes; very fern-like foliage; nodding trusses of rose-red, heart-shaped flowers in late spring to autumn. 'Alba' has white flowers. 30cm (12in).
D. formosa (mountains of California, Oregon). Much like *D. eximia* but the flowers are larger, pink to red, and bloom in spring. Several varieties are listed under this species with flowers in shades of pink or red; 'Bountiful' (deep red, grey-green foliage) is the best known.
D. spectabilis (Japan, Korea, China). Popularly known as bleeding heart, this is a clump-forming, vigorous plant with grey-green, fern-like foliage and rose-crimson, white-tipped, heart-shaped flowers on arching stems in spring. Up to 60cm (2ft).

▽ *Dicentra spectabilis*

DICTAMNUS
(Burning bush)

Generally, only one species is grown – a herbaceous plant of clump-forming habit which produces erect spikes of flowers with long protruding stamens, in summer. It is

Dictamnus albus

Dierama pulcherrimum

usually grown in herbaceous and shrub beds and borders and has aromatic foliage which, especially during hot still weather, gives off a volatile oil which can be ignited.

HOW TO GROW

Grow in fertile, well-drained soil in full sun, although partial shade is tolerated. Plant in autumn or spring.

PROPAGATION

Sow seed when ripe, or lift and divide clumps in spring.

POPULAR SPECIES

D. albus (D. fraxinella) (Italy to Greece, and N. to E. Russia). Pinnate foliage; purple-pink flowers in spikes *(D.a. purpureus)* or white; summer. 40–80cm (1ft 4in–2ft 8in).

DIERAMA
(Wand flower)

These are clump-forming evergreen plants which grow from corms. They have grassy foliage and wiry arching stems bearing thread-like branches and pendulous flowers. They look lovely when planted by a pool.

HOW TO GROW

Grow in fertile, well-drained but moisture-retentive soil, preferably in a sheltered, sunny site. They are not completely hardy

but may be grown under protection in cooler areas. Plant in spring.

PROPAGATION

Divide congested clumps in spring.

POPULAR SPECIES

D. pendulum (S. Africa). Pink, purple or white flowers in summer. 90cm (3ft).
D. pulcherrimum (S. Africa). Much like *D. pendulum* but more robust; purple to dark red flowers; several fine hybrid varieties have been raised between these two species, including 'Hevon', claret; 'Windhover', pale pink. 2m (6ft).

DIGITALIS
(Foxglove)

These stately and much-loved short-lived perennials bear spikes of tubular flowers, usually in early summer. An ideal place to grow foxgloves is in a woodland garden, but failing this, plant bold groups or drifts of them among shrubs. The common foxglove, *D. purpurea*, is an excellent choice for a cottage or cottage-style garden. The blooms are suitable for cutting.

HOW TO GROW

Grow in humus-rich soil (add peat or leaf-mould before planting) in shade or sun; the best results come from soil which does not dry out. Plant in autumn or spring.

▲ *Digitalis purpurea* 'Excelsior'

PROPAGATION

Sow seeds in late spring, outdoors or under the protection of glass.

POPULAR SPECIES

D. ferruginea (S. Europe, from Italy eastwards). Yellow-brown or red-brown flowers; summer. 60–120cm (2–4ft).
D. grandiflora (D. ambigua) (Europe, Caucasus, Siberia). Biennial to perennial; flowers soft yellow, marked brown within; summer. 60–100cm (2–3ft).
D. lutea (W. and W. C. Europe). Like *D. grandiflora* but has paler flowers in summer.
D. × mertonensis. Much like *D. purpurea* but more compact; flowers crushed strawberry-pink; summer. 60–90cm (2–3ft).
D. purpurea (S.W. Europe). Biennial or short-lived perennial; rose or red-purple flowers, maroon-spotted within; summer.

1–1.5m (3–5ft). *D.p. alba* has white flowers; the 'Excelsior' hybrids are popular, with large flowers in many colours.

DORONICUM
(Leopard's bane)

Clump-forming herbaceous plants, widely planted for spring colour. They produce bright yellow daisy-like flowers. Being dwarf plants, the leopard's banes are ideal for the front of herbaceous borders and island beds, perhaps in association with blue-flowered pulmonarias.

HOW TO GROW

Grow in any well-drained but moisture-retentive soil in sun or light shade; growth is poor in soil which dries out. Plant them in the autumn or spring.

▲ *Doronicum orientale* 'Spring Beauty'

PROPAGATION

Divide established clumps at planting time.

POPULAR SPECIES

D. austriacum (mountains of C. and S. Europe). Yellow daisy-like flowers in spring. 45cm (1½ft).

D. columnae (D. cordatum) (E. Alps, Apennines; mountains of Rumania and Balkan Peninsula). Flowers as above. 15–30cm (6–12in).

D. × 'Miss Mason'. Hybrid; flowers as above. 30cm (12in).

▼ *Doronicum plantagineum*

D. orientale (S.E. Europe). Similar to *D. columnae*. 30cm (12in). 'Spring Beauty' has double flowers.

D. plantagineum (W. Europe to N. France). Flowers as above. 80cm (2½ft). Varieties include 'Harpur Crewe' with flowers 7.5cm (3in) across. This is an exceptionally tall variety of *Doronicum*. 1.5m (5ft).

DRACUNCULUS
(Dragon arum)

L atin for little dragon, dracunculus is sometimes grown in gardens for its curiosity value. The arum-like flowers look rather sinister and have a foetid smell. This is a tuberous-rooted plant, and is herbaceous in habit.

HOW TO GROW

Grow in any humus-rich soil, preferably in sun. Plant in late summer to autumn.

PROPAGATION

Detach offsets when dormant, or sow seed when ripe.

POPULAR SPECIES

D. vulgaris (Arum dracunculus) (Mediterranean). Deeply lobed leaves; green-white mottled stem; chocolate-purple spathes; summer. 1m (3ft).

▼ *Dracunculus vulgaris*

▲ *Dryopteris pseudo-mas*

DRYOPTERIS
(Ferns)

O ften known as buckler ferns, these ferns get their name from the appearance of the scales under their leaves. This genus contains evergreen and deciduous species. Both are ideal for planting in cool shady places – for example, in a woodland garden, in a shady courtyard, or among shrubs.

HOW TO GROW
Grow in humus-rich soil in shade or in sun if the soil is sufficiently moist, preferably sheltered from strong winds. Plant in autumn or spring.

PROPAGATION
Divide established clumps at planting time.

POPULAR SPECIES
D. cristata (Europe to S. C. USSR). Popularly known as the crested buckler fern; deciduous; suitable for bog and waterside. 60–100cm (2–3ft).
D. filix-mas (N. temperate zone). Known as the male fern; semi-evergreen to deciduous; several varieties. 1m (3ft).
D. pseudo-mas (temperate zones). Usually evergreen until at least late winter; fronds covered in rusty scales. 1m (3ft).

E
ECHINACEA
(Purple cone flower)

T hese clump-forming herbaceous plants have large daisy-like flower heads in late summer to autumn. They are highly recommended for herbaceous beds and borders; the flowers are good for cutting

HOW TO GROW
Grow in humus-rich, well-drained but moisture-retentive soil in a sunny site. Growth is poor if the soil dries out in summer. Plant in early spring.

PROPAGATION
Divide established clumps at planting time.

POPULAR SPECIES
E. purpurea (Ontario, south to Georgia). Rough-textured, rich green foliage; red-purple flowers with brown cone in centre; late summer to autumn. Several varieties, such as 'Robert Bloom' and 'The King'. 90–120cm (3–4ft).

▼ *Echinacea purpurea* 'Robert Bloom'

ECHINOPS
(Globe thistle)

C lump-forming herbaceous plants with prickly, lobed leaves, they have upright branching stems which carry globe-shaped, spiky flower heads in the summer. Globe thistles are very distinctive plants and contrast with many other perennials in herbaceous borders or beds, especially those with flowers carried in spikes. They are also good with flat-headed perennials, such as the yellow achilleas, and are excellent plants for combining with shrubs – they contrast beautifully with purple-foliage shrubs, for instance, and with shrub roses.

▽ *Echinops humilis*

POPULAR SPECIES

E. bannaticus (S.E. Europe). Triangular-lobed downy leaves, with a few spines; grey-blue flowers; late summer. 1.5m (5ft).
E. humilis (Asia). Similar to *E. ritro*, but leaves almost spineless. 1.2m (4ft). 'Taplow Blue, is a well-known variety, with bright blue flowers; 2m (6ft).
E. ritro (E. Europe to W. Asia). Downy or hairy, lobed and spiny leaves; deep metallic-blue flowers in late summer. The variety 'Veitch's Blue' has a richer flower colour. 60cm (2ft).

EPILOBIUM
(Willow-herb)

The species described here are good herbaceous-border plants and should not be confused with the weeds that are also known as willow-herb. They are dwarf plants with funnel-shaped flowers.

▽ *Epilobium glabellum*

HOW TO GROW

Grow in any well-drained soil in sun, even in very hot dry places. Plant them in the autumn or spring.

PROPAGATION

Divide at planting time, or take root cuttings in winter and plant in a garden frame.

HOW TO GROW

Grow in sun in any well-drained soil that is moderately moisture retentive. Plant in autumn or spring.

PROPAGATION

Divide established clumps in the autumn or the spring.

POPULAR SPECIES

E. dodonaei (C. France to W. Ukraine). This tufted herbaceous plant has narrow leaves and bright pink flowers in summer. 20–100cm (8–36in).

E. glabellum (New Zealand). Not fully hardy, tufted herbaceous plant; narrow leaves, often bronze-flushed; flowers white to cream; summer. 15–30cm (6–12in).

EPIMEDIUM
(Barrenwort)

These are evergreen and deciduous dwarf perennials that spread by rhizomes, forming clumps and colonies which make good ground cover, among shrubs especially, or in woodland gardens. They have attractive fern-like foliage, which is particularly eye-catching in spring when tinted or flushed with shades of pink, copper or red. They also have sprays of pendulous flowers in spring.

HOW TO GROW

Grow in humus-rich soil (add peat or leaf-mould before planting), in partial shade or sun. Plant after flowering, or in autumn.

PROPAGATION

Divide at planting time.

POPULAR SPECIES

E. alpinum (N. and C. Italy to Albania). Deciduous; dark red flowers. 30cm (12in).

E. grandiflorum (E. macranthum) (Japan). Deciduous; flowers are a deep rose to violet or white. Varieties include 'Rose Queen', crimson-pink; 'White Queen', white; 'Violaceum', deep lilac. 30cm (12in).

E. perralderanum (Algeria). Evergreen; bright yellow flowers. 30cm (12in).

E. perralchicum (of garden origin) is a name covering hybrids between *E. pinnatum colchium* and *E. perralderanum.*

E. pinnatum (Iran). Almost evergreen; bright yellow flowers. 30cm (12in).

E. pubigerum (Caucasus, Turkey, Balkan Peninsula). Deciduous; flowers are a pale yellow and pink or white. 45cm (1½ft).

E. × rubrum. Deciduous; leaves strongly tinted red when young; red and white

 *Epimedium × perralchicum*

▽ *Epimedium × rubrum*

▽ *Epimedium × youngianum* 'Niveum'

flowers. 30cm (12in).

E. × versicolor. Deciduous; yellow and pink flowers. 30cm (12in).

E. × warleyense. Deciduous; copper-red and yellow flowers. 30cm (12in).

E. × youngianum. Deciduous; white flowers, tinted with green. 15–25cm (6–10in). The form *E. × y.* 'Niveum' has white flowers and grows compactly. 15cm (6in) high.

ERANTHIS
(Winter aconite)

These perennials flower in late winter and early spring and die back in early summer. They grow from tuber-like rhizomes. They are dwarf plants, ideal for underplanting shrubs and small trees, and bear yellow buttercup-like blooms, each enhanced with a ruff of green leafy bracts. The deeply cut foliage is also attractive.

HOW TO GROW

Grow in humus-rich soil (add peat and leaf-mould before planting) in a sunny or shady spot. Plant in bold groups or drifts for best effect. Plant in early autumn or as soon afterwards as possible.

PROPAGATION

Separate offsets when dormant or divide clumps at flowering time.

Eranthis cilicicus

POPULAR SPECIES

E. cilicicus (Greece to Syria). Deep yellow flowers. 5–7.5cm (2–3in).

E. hyemalis (S.E. France to Bulgaria). Bright yellow flowers. 7.5cm (3in).

E. × tubergenii. A hybrid of the above species with larger flowers and more robust habit. 'Guinea Gold' is the best named variety. 7.5cm (3in).

EREMURUS
(Foxtail lily)

These are large, clump-forming herbaceous plants with tall stately spikes of foxtail-like flowers in summer. They grow from thick fleshy roots and have strap-shaped leaves. They are unusual plants, but not too difficult to grow given the right conditions, and are excellent for the back of a herbaceous or shrub border. The foxtail lilies also make good specimen plants because their habit is sufficiently distinctive for them to stand alone.

HOW TO GROW

Foxtail lilies need a fertile, well-drained soil and grow particularly well in chalky conditions. A very sunny aspect is essential, but preferably sheltered from early morning sun because the young leaves can be damaged by spring frosts. Plant or replant in autumn, but be very careful with the roots

Eremurus stenophyllus

Eremurus robustus elwesii

because, being fleshy, they are easily damaged. An annual mulch of decayed manure or garden compost in spring will maintain vigorous growth.

PROPAGATION

Divide established clumps of foxtail lilies carefully at planting time, or sow from seeds when ripe. However, seedlings take a long time to establish themselves and take at least five years to flower.

POPULAR SPECIES

E. robustus (Turkestan). Peach-pink flowers in summer. 1.5–3m (5–10ft). Varieties are *E.r. elwesii*, pink, late spring to early summer; and *E.* × 'Shelford', a range of hybrid varieties with flowers in shades of yellow to orange-buff, pink and white, in summer. 1.5–2m (5–7ft).

E. stenophyllus (Iran and adjacent USSR). Bright yellow flowers in summer. 60–120cm (2–4ft) high.

Erigeron s. 'Foerster's Liebling'

Erigeron glaucus

Erigeron s. 'Gaiety'

Erigeron mucronatus

ERIGERON
(Fleabane)

These popular clump-forming herbaceous plants have large daisy-like flowers in summer and early autumn. They are generally planted at the front of borders and herbaceous beds because they are dwarf plants. But they also make very good cut flowers.

HOW TO GROW

Grow fleabane in a well-drained, fertile soil in a sunny site. Plant in autumn or spring.

PROPAGATION

Divide at planting time.

POPULAR SPECIES

E. glaucus (California). Evergreen; leaves are glaucous, pink flowers summer to autumn. 15–30cm (5–12in).

E. mucronatus (Mexico). Matt forming species; small white flowers summer to autumn. 10–25 (8–10in).
E. speciosus (W. USA). Lilac to violet flowers in summer. 45–60cm (1½–2ft). There are numerous varieties, which are generally grown rather than the species, such as 'Charity', pink; 'Darkest of All', deep violet-blue; 'Dignity', mauve-blue; 'Gaiety', deep pink; 'Serenity', deep violet; 'Foerster's Liebling', deep pink; 'Dimity', pink.

ERYNGIUM

These herbaceous and evergreen perennials of upright, clump-forming habit have sword-, or strap- to heart-shaped leaves, often deeply lobed and spiny. Small, purple to blue, or green-white flowers are carried in large globe-shaped heads, each surrounded by conspicuous leafy bracts, in

▲ *Eryngium alpinum*

early summer to early autumn. They are excellent plants for combining with shrubs in the mixed border, ideal for herbaceous beds and borders, and a good choice for planting in gravel areas or in the vicinity of a patio.

HOW TO GROW
Grow in well-drained soil in a sunny situation. Plant eryngium in the early autumn or in the spring.

PROPAGATION
Divide carefully in the spring, when possible; or plant root cuttings in late winter.

POPULAR SPECIES
E. alpinum (Jura, Alps and mountains W. and C. Yugoslavia). Clump-forming; semi-evergreen; blue flower heads surrounded by feathery, spiny, metallic-blue bracts, summer to early autumn. 75cm (2½ft).
E. amethystinum (Italy, Sicily to Balkan Peninsula). Semi-evergreen; spiny leaves; blue flower heads surrounded by spiny amethyst bracts. 45–60cm (1½–2ft).

▲ *Eryngium amethystinum*
▼ *Eryngium bourgatii*

E. bourgatii (Pyrenees). White-veined spiny leaves; blue-green flower heads, summer to early autumn. 60cm (2ft).

E. maritimum (Europe). Popularly known as sea holly; deciduous; spiny blue-grey leaves; blue flower heads, summer to early autumn. 30cm (12in).

E. planum (C. and S.E. Europe). Semi-evergreen; light blue flower heads, green-blue spiny bracts. 60–90cm (2–3ft).

E. variifolium (Morocco). Evergreen; glossy green leaves with white veins, in flat rosettes; grey-blue flower heads, late summer. 45cm (1½ft).

Eryngium maritimum

ERYSIMUM
(Siberian wallflower)

The plants described here are short-lived perennials, rather like a small wallflower; indeed the erysimums are related to wallflowers. They can be used for bedding, like wallflowers, but look equally good planted in mixed borders, herbaceous beds and even in a rock garden.

HOW TO GROW

Erysimums need a well-drained soil although it can be poor in nutrients. Plant in a sunny spot, sheltered from cold drying winds. Plant in early autumn.

Erysimum × allionii

PROPAGATION

Raise from seeds sown outside in late spring or early summer.

POPULAR SPECIES

E. × allionii. A hybrid, and a short-lived perennial, best raised regularly from seeds. Bushy upright habit; bright orange flowers, in spring to summer. 30cm (12in) or more.

E. alpinum (Cheiranthus alpinus) (N. Europe). Dark green leaves, bright yellow fragrant flowers, early summer. 25cm (10in).

EUPATORIUM
(Hemp agrimony)

These are herbaceous perennials with large heads of groundsel-like flowers in summer and autumn. They are useful plants for a herbaceous bed or border, or for a mixed border, and a good choice, too, for an informal cottage garden.

HOW TO GROW

Grow in any well-drained but moisture-retentive soil in sun or light shade. Growth will be rather poor if the soil dries out in the summer. Plant in autumn or spring.

PROPAGATION

Divide established clumps at planting time, or from seed in the spring.

POPULAR SPECIES

E. purpureum (E. USA). Purple-rose to magenta-crimson flower heads in autumn; attractive purple stalks. 'Atropurpureum' has attractive purple leaves and pink-mauve flowers. 2–3m (6–10ft).

Eupatorium purpureum

inconspicuous. The heads of bracts generally last for some considerable time.

HOW TO GROW

Spurges (at least most of them) need a well-drained soil in full sun although some will thrive in shade or moist conditions. Plant in autumn or spring.

PROPAGATION

Lift and divide established clumps in spring; or plant basal cuttings at that time.

POPULAR SPECIES

E. characias (Portugal, Mediterranean). Evergreen; large distinctive perennial; grey-green leaves; yellow-green heads in spring.

Euphorbia characias

Euphorbia griffithii

EUPHORBIA
(Spurge)

A large group of plants, containing some very attractive and useful perennial kinds. Some are large, distinctive plants which can be used as specimens, particularly in the vicinity of a patio. Others are ideal for a mixed border in association with shrubs; or for a herbaceous border or bed where they contrast well with many other perennials. The colour comes from the bracts (modified leaves) and not from the flowers, which are small and quite

60–180cm (2–6ft). *E.c. wulfenii (E. wulfenii)*
(E. Mediterranean); more robust than the
type; leaves brighter grey-green; heads
green-yellow.
E. epithymoides (E. polychroma) (C. and S.
Europe). Dwarf clump-forming herbaceous
plant for herbaceous beds and borders;
bright green leaves; brilliant yellow heads in
spring. 30–60cm (1–2ft).
E. griffithii (Himalaya). Herbaceous clump-
forming plant; light red heads in summer.
90cm (3ft). Variety 'Fireglow' has bright,
brick-red heads.
E. myrsinites (S. Europe to W. Turkey).
Evergreen; prostrate stems carrying blue-
grey leaves; bright yellow heads in spring.
Ideal for rock garden. 15cm (6in).

▼ *Euphorbia characias wulfenii*

▲ *Euphorbia epithymoides*

F

FESTUCA
(Fescue grass)

These highly ornamental dwarf grasses form clumps of very thin evergreen leaves. They are excellent for grouping around shrubs for contrast in shape and

▲ *Festuca glauca*

▲ *Filipendula palmata*

foliage colour and useful, too, in herbaceous beds and borders, in gravel areas and for planting in gaps in paving.

HOW TO GROW
Grow in any well-drained soil in sunny positions. Plant in autumn or spring.

PROPAGATION
Divide established clumps at planting time.

POPULAR SPECIES
F. glauca (F. ovina glauca) (Europe). This is the popular blue fescue, with blue-grey foliage. 30cm (12in).

FILIPENDULA

These are herbaceous perennials with attractive compound leaves and large 'frothy' heads of flowers in summer. All but *F. vulgaris* are ideally suited to bog garden or poolside planting. They can also be grown in moist beds and borders.

HOW TO GROW
Grow in any moisture-retentive, but not waterlogged, soil in sun or partial shade. Plant in autumn or spring.

PROPAGATION
Lift and divide established clumps in the autumn or spring.

POPULAR SPECIES
F. palmata (Siberia). Dark green leaves, hairy underneath. Pink flowers. 1m (3ft).
F. ulmaria (Europe, W. Asia). Popularly known as meadow sweet; creamy-white flowers; 'Aurea' has golden foliage. 90–120cm (3–4ft).
F. vulgaris (Europe to Siberia and N. Africa). Known as dropwort; creamy-white flowers. 60cm (2ft) or more; 'Plena' has double flowers.

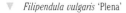
Filipendula ulmaria 'Aurea'

Filipendula vulgaris 'Plena'

G

GAILLARDIA
(Blanket flower)

These are tufted herbaceous perennials which produce large, brightly coloured, daisy-like flowers in summer and early autumn. The flowers are excellent for cutting. They are almost 'essential' plants for herbaceous borders and beds; they can also be grown in mixed borders and are a good choice for cottage gardens.

HOW TO GROW
Grow in ordinary, well-drained soil in a sunny position. Plant in early autumn or spring.

PROPAGATION
Lift and divide established clumps at planting time, or raise from seed in spring.

POPULAR SPECIES
G. aristata (N.C. and N.W. USA). Grey-green downy foliage; large flowers, yellow, sometimes purple-red at base of petals, purple centre. 45–60cm (1½–2ft). Varieties include 'Dazzler', in bright orange-yellow.
G. pulchella (C. and S. USA, Mexico). Similar to *G. aristata* but red-purple flowers with or without small yellow tips. Several varieties are offered in shades of yellow, bronze and red. 45cm (1½ft).

Gaillardia aristata 'Dazzler'

GENTIANA
(Gentian)

These generally tufted perennials have funnel- or bell-shaped flowers, often in beautiful shades of pure blue. The gentians are variable in habit, some being tall plants suitable for herbaceous or mixed borders; others are dwarf kinds ideally suited to rock gardens or peat beds.

HOW TO GROW

Grow in well-drained but moisture-retentive soil. It should be rich in humus, so add plenty of peat or leaf-mould before planting. Some species need an acid or lime-free soil. Generally choose a sunny site, although some species will thrive in partial shade. Plant in spring.

▲ *Gentiana asclepiadea*

▼ *Gentiana lutea*

PROPAGATION

Divide carefully at planting time or plant basal cuttings in the spring. Sow seeds as soon as they are ripe.

POPULAR SPECIES

G. acaulis (Alps, Carpathians to N.E. Spain, C. Italy, C. Yugoslavia). Known as the trumpet gentian; deep blue flowers, spring. 7.5cm (3in).
G. asclepiadea (Alps, N. Apennines). Known as the willow gentian; deep blue flowers, summer to autumn. 60cm (2ft) or more.
G. lutea (mountains of C. and S. Europe). Great yellow gentian; yellow flowers in clusters, in tiered spikes, summer. Up to 1.2m (4ft) tall.
G. septemfida (Turkey to Iran). Purple-blue flowers in summer. 15–30cm (6–12in).
G. sino-ornata (W. China, Tibet). Prostrate habit, bright blue tubular flowers, autumn. Must have acid soil. 15cm (6in).
G. verna (Europe to Arctic Russia). Spring gentian; deep brilliant blue flowers in spring. 7.5cm (3in). *G.v. angulosa* is more robust with larger flowers.

GERANIUM
(Crane's bill)

Clump-forming herbaceous perennials, geraniums have rounded, lobed leaves and a long season of bowl- or saucer-shaped flowers in summer. Being of dwarf habit they are ideal for the front of mixed borders, where they associate well with shrubs, and they should be included in every cottage garden and herbaceous bed or border. Today, many people use some of the geraniums for ground cover among shrubs, under trees, etc.

HOW TO GROW

Geraniums thrive in any well-drained soil, and do not mind dry conditions too much. They can be grown in full sun or partial shade. Plant in autumn or spring.

PROPAGATION

Lift and divide established clumps at planting time.

▲ *Geranium himalayense*

▼ *Geranium macrorrhizum*

POPULAR SPECIES

G. × 'Claridge Druce'. Fairly large purple-pink flowers. At least 45cm (1½ft).

G. endressii (S.W. France and adjacent Spain). Deeply lobed leaves; large flowers, pale pink, summer to autumn. 30–45cm (1–1½ft). Several varieties, including 'A.T. Johnson', silvery pink; and 'Wargrave Pink', bright salmon-pink.

G. himalayense (G. grandiflorum) (Sikkim). Rich violet-blue flowers in early summer. 30–45cm (1–1½ft).

G. macrorrhizum (Balkan Peninsula, Carpathians, S. Alps, Apennines). Deeply lobed leaves; aromatic foliage; purple-red flowers in early summer, white in *G. m.* 'Album'. 20–40cm (8–16in). Excellent ground cover under trees.

G. × *magnificum (G. ibericum)*. Deeply lobed leaves; violet-blue flowers in summer. 45–60cm (1½–2ft).

G. pratense (Europe). Known as meadow crane's bill. Violet-blue flowers in summer. 45–60cm (1½–2ft). Lots of varieties, including double-flowered ones, and the popular 'Johnson's Blue'.

G. wallichianum (Himalaya). Violet-blue flowers, in late summer to autumn. 'Buxton's Blue' is a deeper blue. 60cm (2ft).

GEUM
(Avens)

These are very popular herbaceous plants for cottage gardens, mixed and herbaceous borders. The pinnate foliage is quite attractive, and in summer very brightly coloured, single rose-like flowers are freely produced. They are quite vigorous plants and soon form dense clumps.

HOW TO GROW

Geums will grow in any well-drained but moisture-retentive soil. Growth is not so good in soils which dry out in the summer. They will grow equally well in full sun or light shade. Plant in autumn or spring.

PROPAGATION

Lift and divide established clumps in the autumn or spring.

POPULAR SPECIES

G. × *borisii.* This is a well-known and very popular hybrid with bright, clear orange flowers in early summer; excellent for cottage gardens. 30cm (12in).

G. chiloense (G. coccineum) (Chile). Scarlet flowers in early summer. 60cm (2ft). Usually grown are the larger, double-flowered varieties such as 'Fire Opal', rich bronze-scarlet; 'Lady Stratheden', yellow; 'Mrs Bradshaw', bright brick-red; 'Prince of Orange', rich bronze-scarlet.

G. montanum (mountains of C. and S. Europe). Called mountain avens, this is ideal for rock gardens or the front of small borders; golden-yellow flowers in summer. 15cm (6in).

G. rivale (N. Hemisphere). Known as water avens; nodding bell-shaped flowers, orange-pink, early summer to autumn. 30–45cm (1–1½ft).

▼ *Geum chiloense* 'Prince of Orange'

GYPSOPHILA
(Chalk plant)

The well-loved gypsophila produces 'clouds' of tiny white flowers in summer which make a marvellous foil for brightly or strongly coloured perennials. It also looks good in shrub borders, perhaps in association with purple-leaved shrubs, or with shrub roses, both old and modern. The flowers are excellent for cutting (often arranged with sweet peas).

HOW TO GROW

This is an excellent perennial for chalky soils; however, any well-drained soil is suitable. A site which receives plenty of sun is recommended. Plant in autumn or spring.

PROPAGATION

Propagate from soft basal cuttings in the spring. Do not attempt to lift and divide plants.

POPULAR SPECIES

G. paniculata (C. Europe to C. Asia). Tiny white flowers in summer. 90–120cm (3–4ft). Several varieties are available including 'Bristol Fairy', pure white double; 'Flamingo', double pale pink; 'Rosy Veil', double rose-pink, much shorter than the species.

▼ *Gypsophila paniculata* 'Bristol Fairy'

H

HAKONECHLOA
(Ornamental grass)

There is only one species grown, which spreads by means of rhizomes or underground stems, forming colonies. It is a valuable addition to a mixed or shrub border and for gravel areas in association with other ornamental grasses.

△ *Hakonechloa macra* 'Aureola'

HOW TO GROW
Grow in any well-drained but not dry soil, preferably in partial shade. Plant in spring.

PROPAGATION
Lift and divide established clumps in spring.

POPULAR SPECIES
H. macra (mountains of Japan). Slender, pointed leaves, about 25cm (10in) in length. More attractive are the varieties: *H. m.* 'Albo-aurea', white and yellow variegated, often with an overall bronze hue; *H. m.* 'Albo-variegata', green with white lines.

HELENIUM
(Sneezeweed)

Heleniums are seen in almost every herbaceous bed or border because they flower profusely in summer and autumn and the blooms are highly suitable for cutting. The flowers are daisy-like with prominent domed centres and come in a range of bright colours. A particularly attractive combination consists of groups of heleniums around shrubs noted for autumn leaf colour and/or berries. They are indispensable plants for cottage gardens, combined with, for instance, Michaelmas daisies.

HOW TO GROW
Heleniums grow in any well-drained but moisture-retentive soil in a sunny position.

△ *Helenium autumnale* 'Coppelia'

▽ *Helenium autumnale*

▲ *Helenium autumnale* 'Wyndley'

▲ *Helianthus × multiflorus*

Growth is poor and stunted, however, if the soil is prone to drying out in the summer. Plant in autumn or spring.

PROPAGATION

Lift and divide at planting time.

POPULAR SPECIES

H. autumnale (USA). Herbaceous in habit; clump-forming; yellow flowers. 1.5m (5ft). The species itself is not usually grown, but rather the varieties, of which there is quite a good selection: 'Bruno', mahogany-red, 1m (3ft); 'Butterpat', rich yellow, 1m (3ft); 'Coppelia', coppery-orange, 1m (3ft); 'Pumilum Magnificum', clear yellow, 75cm (2½ft); 'Wyndley', yellow, flecked with orange-brown, 75cm (2½ft).

HELIANTHUS
(Sunflower)

Like the well-known annual sunflowers, the perennial kinds have large, yellow, daisy-like flowers, but they do not attain the size of dinner plates, as do those of the annuals. Most of the perennials are tall, back-of-the-border plants and are suitable for both herbaceous and shrub borders. They are ideal, too, for cottage gardens. The daisy-like flowers combine well with spiky perennials such as delphiniums and also with globe-shaped flowers such as eryngiums and echinops. Sunflowers combine effectively with purple-leaved shrubs, particularly the varieties of *Cotinus coggygria,* or smoke bush. Try them with grey-foliage perennials as well, such as some of the artemisias.

HOW TO GROW

The perennial sunflowers are easily grown in any well-drained soil, but it should not be prone to drying out, otherwise growth may be poor and stunted. A position in full sun is needed. Plant in autumn or spring.

PROPAGATION

Divide established clumps at planting time.

POPULAR SPECIES

H. decapetalus (E. USA). Pale yellow flowers up to 7.5cm (3in) across; summer. 1–1.5m (3–5ft). Its hybrid, *H. × multiflorus,* which is somewhat larger and more robust, is usually grown. Good varieties of this are 'Capenoch Star', light yellow; 'Loddon Gold', double rich yellow; and 'Triomphe de Gard', semi-double clear yellow.

H. salicifolius (S.E. USA). Yellow flowers 5cm (2in) across, with purple-brown centres; early autumn. 1–2m (3–6ft).

Helichrysum italicum

HELICHRYSUM

One species which is commonly grown, the curry plant, is a half-hardy perennial and somewhat shrubby plant which is valued for its aromatic silver foliage. It is an ideal subject for cottage gardens, but can also be grown at the front of herbaceous and shrub borders.

HOW TO GROW

Only suitable for growing outdoors all the year round in mild areas; in colder gardens, overwinter the plant under the protection of glass. For helichrysums to do well they must have a very sheltered spot with full sun and well-drained soil. Plant in spring.

PROPAGATION

Take cuttings and plant them in the spring or summer.

POPULAR SPECIES

H. italicum (H. angustifolium, H. serotinum) (S. Europe). Narrow, silvery, foliage with a strong smell of curry. In summer this plant bears clusters of small deep yellow flowers. 60cm (2ft) when in flower.

Helictotrichon sempervirens

HELICTOTRICHON
(Ornamental grass)

This is a clump-forming grass with superb foliage and indeed one of the most popular of the ornamental kinds. It has several uses and associates well with many other plants, both perennials and shrubs. It looks good with paving, so try it in patio beds. Group it with purple-foliage shrubs, or with red or pink shrub roses. Combine it with daisy-flowered perennials, especially those with yellow blooms. It is an excellent choice, too, for cottage-garden borders, and also for planting in gravel areas in association with other ornamental grasses.

HOW TO GROW

Grow in any well-drained soil, preferably in sun, although light shade is tolerated. Plant in spring.

PROPAGATION

Divide established clumps in spring.

POPULAR SPECIES

H. sempervirens (Avena sempervirens, A. candida) (S.W. Europe). Clump-forming, with thin, arching, grey-green leaves up to 45cm (1½ft) long; the flowering stems (also known as panicles) reach 1.2m (4ft) high in summer.

Heliopsis h. scabra 'Golden Plume'

HELIOPSIS

These plants are rather like perennial sunflowers, with yellow daisy-like blooms in summer or early autumn. They have the same uses as sunflowers.

HOW TO GROW

They are easily grown in any well-drained soil, but it should not be prone to drying out, otherwise growth may be poor and stunted. A position in full sun is needed. Plant in autumn or spring.

PROPAGATION

Divide established clumps at planting time.

POPULAR SPECIES

H. helianthoides (E. USA). A clump-forming

herbaceous perennial with yellow flowers in autumn. Up to 1.5m (5ft) tall. Varieties of *H.h. scabra (H. scabra)* are normally grown, such as 'Gigantea', larger than the species, deep yellow; 'Golden Plume', double orange-yellow, 1m (3ft); 'Goldgreenheart', double chrome-yellow, green-yellow centre; 'Incomparabilis', almost fully double, orange, zinnia-like.

HELLEBORUS
(Hellebore)

This is a group of highly distinctive, 'aristocratic' evergreen and deciduous perennials. Often the foliage is very attractive in itself. Cup- or bowl-shaped flowers are produced, mainly in winter or spring, depending on the species. Some kinds are clump-forming, with leaves springing mainly from ground level; others are tufted and somewhat shrub-like, with leaves carried on erect biennial stems.

The hellebores are ideal for planting in bold groups in shrub borders, because they associate particularly well with shrubs. They are ideal, too, for woodland gardens.

HOW TO GROW
Grow in any well-drained, limy, preferably humus-rich soil (add peat or leaf-mould), in sun or light shade. Plant in autumn or after flowering. Do not disturb hellebores unless it is absolutely necessary, because they prefer to be left alone.

PROPAGATION
Divide carefully immediately after flowering; or sow seed as soon as it is ripe. Seedlings take two or three years to flower.

POPULAR SPECIES
H. atrorubens (garden origin). Clump-forming; flowers bowl-shaped, red-purple, shaded green; winter. 30–45cm (1–1½ft).
H. foetidus (W. Europe). Commonly known as the stinking hellebore; a shrub-like plant with attractive foliage and nodding, pale green, cup-shaped flowers in winter and spring. Up to 75cm (2½ft).
H. lividus (Majorca). Shrub-like plant; deep

▲ *Helleborus foetidus*

▼ *Helleborus lividus corsicus*

glossy green leaves with white veins; bowl-shaped yellow-green flowers, spring. Not reliably hardy (needs a warm spot). 30cm (12in) or more. *H.l. corsicus (H. corsicus, H. argutifolius)* has glossy leaves with spiny edges, and bright yellow-green flowers. 60cm (24in).
H. niger (E. Alps, Apennines). This is the

▲ *Helleborus orientalis* hybrid

▼ *Helleborus niger*

well-loved Christmas rose, a clump-forming plant with bowl-shaped white flowers in winter (sometimes at Christmas-time). A good variety is 'Potter's Wheel' with flowers 10cm (4in) or more wide. 30cm (12in).

H. orientalis (Greece, Turkey). One of the most popular hellebores and ideal for shrub borders or woodland gardens. Bowl-shaped, creamy-white flowers, on stems up to 60cm (2ft) tall; spring. There are many hybrids under this name with flowers in shades of purple, pink, cream and white.

H. viridis (W. and N.W. Europe). Known as the green hellebore; a clump-forming plant with coarsely toothed leaves and deep green flowers in winter and spring. Try grouping this species with snowdrops *(Galanthus)* for a striking effect.

HEMEROCALLIS
(Day lily)

These plants are herbaceous perennials in the lily family and do indeed have large, lily-like flowers, in the summer and through to autumn. Each flower lasts for only one day, hence the common name, but the plants produce a long succession of them. They are clump-forming plants with long, narrow, arching leaves, which are quite attractive. Hemerocallis have many uses: of course, they are ideal for herbaceous borders or island beds; they look even better in a shrub border because they contrast well in colour

▼ *Hemerocallis fulva*

▲ *Hemerocallis* 'Golden Chimes'

Japan). Fragrant orange-yellow flowers in early summer. 30cm (12in) or more.

There are scores of named hybrid varieties, raised in Britain and the USA. They usually have larger flowers and all are easy to grow. Popular varieties include: 'Bonanza', pale orange with claret centre; 'Golden Orchid', with rich yellow flowers; 'Morocco Red', deep red with a yellow centre; 'Pink Damask', orange-pink with a yellow centre; and 'Pink Prelude', pink with a yellow centre.

HESPERIS
(Dame's violet, sweet rocket)

The species grown is a popular cottage-garden perennial with flowers which are very fragrant in the evening during summer. Mix it with other summer flowers and make sure it is near to a sitting area where its fragrance can be easily enjoyed.

HOW TO GROW

Grow in any well-drained, preferably humus-rich and limy soil in sun or light shade. Plant in autumn or spring.

PROPAGATION

Propagate from seed when ripe or in spring; propagate double flowering types by cuttings or careful division in spring.

POPULAR SPECIES

H. matronalis (Europe, Asia). The four-

▼ *Hesperis matronalis*

and form with so many shrubs. They are also almost 'essential' plants for the edge of a woodland garden and no self-respecting cottage garden should be without some clumps of day lilies. Patio gardeners should be pleased to learn that day lilies make excellent tub plants.

HOW TO GROW

Day lilies grow well in any ordinary well-drained soil but it should be rich in humus (add peat or leaf-mould before planting) and moisture retentive. They flourish near the edge of a pool. Position them in full sun for optimum flowering. Plant these plants in the autumn or spring.

PROPAGATION

Divide established clumps at planting time.

POPULAR SPECIES

H. fulva (Europe to Siberia). Buff-orange flowers in summer. Up to 1m (3ft).
H. lilioasphodelus (H. flava) (S.E. Europe to Siberia). Clear yellow fragrant flowers, spring. 60–90cm (2–3ft).
H. middendorfii (E. Asia, including Korea,

petalled flowers are lilac-purple and are produced on spikes during the summer. 75–120cm (2½–4ft). Varieties include 'Candidissima' ('Nivea'), white; double-flowered forms in white and purple occur but unfortunately are not easy to obtain.

HEUCHERA
(Coral flower)

These are tufted evergreen perennials with quite attractive rounded leaves and sprays of tiny flowers in the summer. They are traditional cottage-garden plants, but are also worthwhile additions to modern herbaceous borders and island beds.

HOW TO GROW
Grow in well-drained humus-rich soil in sun or light shade. Plant after flowering in autumn, or spring.

PROPAGATION
Lift and divide established clumps in the autumn or spring.

POPULAR SPECIES
H. × *brizoides.* A group of hybrids with flowers that range from near white ('Pearl Drops'), and light crimson ('Coral Cloud'), to salmon-scarlet with bronze foliage ('Splendour'). 45cm (1½ft).
H. sanguinea (S.W. USA, mountains of Mexico). Somewhat marbled leaves; crimson to scarlet flowers in early summer. 30–60cm (1–2ft). Several good varieties include 'Red Spangles' which is a bright red, and 'Scintillation' which is pink tinged with a little orange.

▼ *Heuchera* 'Red Spangles'

island beds. They are also suitable for cottage gardens.

HOW TO GROW

Grow in any well-drained humus-rich soil in sun or shade. They are more shade-tolerant than *Heuchera*. Plant after flowering, in autumn or spring.

PROPAGATION

Lift and divide established clumps in the autumn or the spring.

POPULAR SPECIES

(In this instance, they are not species but hybrids.)

× *H. alba* 'Bridget Bloom'. Clump-forming plant with dainty sprays of light pink flowers, summer. 45cm (1½ft).

× *H. tiarelloides*. A spreading plant which carries 30cm (12in) tall sprays of tiny, salmon-pink bells in early summer.

HOSTA
(Plantain lily)

The hostas are probably the most dramatic of all the foliage herbaceous perennials, with their large leaves in many shades of green, blue-grey, yellow or gold, and variegated green and white. They do flower, producing spikes of mainly lilac, mauve or white lily-like flowers in the summer, but most are essentially foliage plants.

The hostas make excellent ground cover in the summer with their dense canopy of foliage, especially if mass planted. They contrast in colour, shape and texture with so many other plants. For instance, group them with shrubs in a mixed border or in a woodland garden with rhododendrons, candelabra primulas and blue poppies. Group them with ferns, ivies and other shade-loving plants in a cool corner of a patio or courtyard. Have bold groups beside a garden pool. Even grow them in ornamental containers such as wooden or terracotta tubs.

HOW TO GROW

Grow in moisture-retentive, preferably

△ × *Heucherella alba* 'Bridget Bloom'

× HEUCHERELLA

This plant is a cross between *Heuchera*, the coral flower, and *Tiarella* and spreads widely. The hybrids blend the characteristics of the parents and are attractive plants for herbaceous borders or

▲ *Hosta fortunei hyacinthina*

▼ *Hosta sieboldiana elegans*

POPULAR SPECIES

(From Japan, unless stated otherwise).
H. albo-marginata. White-edged leaves up to 15cm (6in) long; pale violet flowers.
H. crispula. Wavy white-edged leaves about 20cm (8in) long; lavender flowers.
H. fortunei. Leaves 15cm (6in) long, plain green; flowers lilac to violet. There are many varieties, such as 'Albopicta', yellow, green-edged leaves; 'Aurea', yellow foliage; and *H. f. hyacinthina*, grey-green leaves; red-violet flowers. Many more besides.
H. × 'Honey Bells'. Green foliage; grown for its fragrant white flowers. 1m (3ft).
H. lancifolia. Slender pointed, glossy green leaves to 20cm (8in); deep purple flowers.
H. plantaginea (China). Leaves 25cm (10in) long, lustrous pale green; pure white, scented flowers. *H.p. grandiflora* is larger and an even better choice.
H. sieboldiana (H. glauca). A robust species with leaves more than 30cm (12in) long, grey-green; pale lilac flowers. *H.s. elegans* has leaves which are more intensely grey-green.
H. 'Thomas Hogg'. Similar to *H. crispula*, but

▼ *Hosta plantaginea*

humus-rich soil (add peat or leaf-mould before planting), in light shade or sun. Plant in autumn or spring. Maintain slug pellets around the plants as soon as they start into growth because slugs and snails can cause considerable foliage damage.

PROPAGATION
Lift and divide clumps at planting time.

leaves less waved and pointed.
H. undulata (H. lancifolia undulata). White-splashed leaves about 15cm (6in) long; pale violet to lavender flowers.
H. ventricosa. Leaves about 25cm (10in) long, deep, somewhat glossy green; deep violet flowers. Variety 'Aureomaculata' has yellow-centred leaves; the leaves of 'Variegata' have yellow edges.

INCARVILLEA

This is a clump-forming perennial with attractive pinnate foliage and flamboyant funnel-shaped flowers in early summer. It is an easily grown but unusual subject for the edge of a shrub border or woodland garden, or for herbaceous borders or island beds. It also associates particularly well with shrubs.

HOW TO GROW

Grow in well-drained, humus-rich soil (add plenty of peat or leaf-mould before planting), and in sun or light shade. Preferably planted in spring, when it establishes itself best.

PROPAGATION

Divide established clumps or raise from seed under glass in spring. Seedlings take two to four years to flower.

POPULAR SPECIES

I. delavayi (China). Compound leaves up to 30cm (12in) long; bright purple-rose flowers with a yellow throat, in early summer. 45–60cm (1½–2ft).
I. grandiflora (China). Pinnale leaves; deep pink flowers early summer. 30 cm (12in).

Incarvillea delavayi

INULA

These distinctive, aristocratic, clump-forming perennials have attractive bold foliage and upright stems of yellow daisy-like flowers in late summer. They are plants for moist soils and look especially good near a pool, or at the edge of a woodland garden. They are also a superb choice for a shrub border because they contrast superbly with many shrubs, both in form and colour.

HOW TO GROW

Grow in moisture-retentive but well-drained soil, preferably high in humus (add peat or leaf-mould before planting), in a sunny spot. Plant in autumn or spring.

▼ *Inula hookeri*

PROPAGATION

Divide established clumps, or sow seeds, in the spring.

POPULAR SPECIES

I. ensifolia (E. and C. Europe to Caucasus). Yellow flowers on stems about 30cm (12in), late summer.
I. helenium (probably C. Asia to S.E. Europe but much naturalized elsewhere). Popularly called elecampane. Bright yellow flowers, summer. 2m (6ft).
I. hookeri (Himalaya). Light yellow flowers, late summer. 60cm (2ft).
I. magnifica (Caucasus). Deep bright yellow. 2m (6ft).
I. orientalis (I. glandulosa) (Caucasus). Orange-yellow. 45cm (1½ft) or more.

IRIS

This is a huge group of plants, some of which are bulbous, others (the perennial kinds) spread by rhizomes (thick underground stems). The perennial species form bold clumps or tufts of sword-like or grassy, often evergreen, foliage, and, mainly in summer, produce spikes of flamboyant flowers, generally composed of horizontally flared and upright petals.

The best-loved of all irises are the bearded hybrids which flower in early summer. They should be in every herbaceous border or island bed, and they look particularly lovely when grouped with lupins, paeonies and Oriental poppies. The bearded irises also look good among shrubs in a mixed border. The species described here are recommended for both herbaceous and shrub borders. The flowers are often used for cutting and arranging in water.

HOW TO GROW

Irises thrive in any well-drained soil and are especially good for chalky or limy soils. They appreciate a moderately fertile soil. Best flowering is achieved when the plants are positioned in full sun, although partial shade is acceptable. The species are planted in autumn or spring; but the bearded hybrids are ideally planted immediately after flowering in early summer.

PROPAGATION

Lift and divide established clumps at planting time. Each division should consist of some rhizome, with fibrous roots attached, and one or more 'fans' of leaves.

▲ *Iris unguicularis*

▼ *Iris foetidissima*, in fruit

POPULAR SPECIES

Bearded hybrids. The best-known of all irises, their flowers embrace all the colours of the rainbow. A vast range of varieties is available and new ones appear on the market each year. All are good garden plants and the choice of varieties has to be a personal one – choose colours that appeal to you. There are tall bearded irises, 90cm (3ft) or more in height; intermediate varieties, 25–60cm (10 to 24in) tall; and dwarf varieties, up to 23cm

▲ *Iris pallida* 'Aurea-variegata'

▼ *Iris pumila* 'Pogo'

(9in) high. They are called bearded irises because they have a 'beard' of a contrasting colour at the base of each lower petal.

I. foetidissima (W. Europe to N. Africa). Popularly known as the gladwin. Narrow grassy foliage; flowers are purple-grey to mauve or yellow; seeds are bright orange-red, very showy in autumn. Useful for shady spots. 45cm (1½ft).

I. pallida (S.E. Europe). Fragrant lavender-blue flowers; early summer; sword-like grey-green leaves. 75cm (2½ft). *I.p. dalmatica* 'Aurea-variegata' has yellow-striped leaves, and those of *I.p.d.* 'Variegata' are striped creamy white.

I. pumila (I. attica) (C. Europe to S. USSR, and Turkey). A dwarf iris with 20cm (8in) long leaves and stemless straw-yellow flowers in spring. There are several colour

forms, with flowers from deep to pale yellow and in shades of purple and blue.

I. unguicularis (I. stylosa) (Greece and Algeria, east to Syria). The Algerian or winter iris has deep green grassy foliage and fragrant, bright, deep lilac flowers from late autumn to spring during mild spells. 'Alba' has white flowers. Up to 30cm (12in).

K

KNIPHOFIA
(Red-hot poker)

Most of the red-hot pokers are evergreen perennials from Africa. The mainly hardy South African species recommended here are clump-forming or tufted plants with handsome grassy or long sword-shaped leaves. The bold spikes of tubular flowers appear mainly in late summer and autumn.

These are stately, 'architectural' plants, associating particularly well with modern architecture and paving, so are ideal subjects for providing an exotic touch to a patio. Red-hot pokers also look superb planted in a gravel area with other plants such as yuccas, phormiums and ornamental grasses. Red-hot pokers are also traditionally grown in cottage gardens.

They can, of course, also be grown in herbaceous borders or island beds, where they combine well with perennials that have flat heads of flowers, such as some of the achilleas. They flower in early autumn, so try combining them, too, with Michaelmas daisies *(Aster)* and with *Sedum spectabile.*

▼ *Kniphofia caulescens*

▲ *Kniphofia galpinii*

Kniphofias are magnificent in shrub or mixed borders and combine well with shrubs which are noted for their autumn leaf colour and/or berries.

HOW TO GROW

Grow in well-drained but moisture-retentive, preferably humus-rich soil, in sun. In very cold areas the plants may need protection in winter, by covering the crowns with straw or bracken. In any area it is the usual practice, in late autumn, to tie up leaves into a wigwam, so that the plants' crowns are protected from excessive rain which can rot them. Plant in spring.

PROPAGATION

Lift and divide established clumps in spring.

POPULAR SPECIES

K. caulescens. Striking grey-green leaves up to 90cm (3ft) long; light salmon-red flowers, which yellow with age; autumn. 1–1.5m (3–5ft).
K. galpinii. Grassy foliage; bright red-orange flowers; autumn. 75cm (2½ft).
K. uvaria. Handsome leaves up to 90cm (3ft); scarlet flowers, ageing to yellow; autumn. 1.2–1.5m (4–5ft).
In addition to the species there are many hybrid varieties with flowers in various other colours, such as yellow and cream.

L

LAMIASTRUM
(Yellow archangel)

This is an excessively vigorous, prostrate, ground-cover plant, ideal for shade. It should not be considered in small gardens, where it could take over a border (although it is easily 'controlled' by digging it out), but is ideal for covering extensive areas in the larger garden, say among large shrubs or under trees, or for clothing steep banks.

HOW TO GROW

Grow in any well-drained soil in sun or shade. Plant in autumn or spring.

PROPAGATION

Lift and divide at planting time.

POPULAR SPECIES

L. galeobdolon (L. luteum, Galeobdolon luteum, Lamium galeobdolon) (Europe). This is the only species. Its variety *L.g.* 'Variegatum', has oval evergreen leaves which are attractively splashed with silver, and spikes of yellow flowers, in spring. 30cm (12in) high.

▼ *Lamiastrum galeobdolon* 'Variegatum'

LAMIUM
(Dead-nettle)

These are tufted or clump-forming but low-spreading ground-cover plants, with evergreen foliage and spikes of flowers in spring or summer. They are ideal for ground cover in smaller gardens, in a shrub border, for example.

HOW TO GROW
Grow in any well-drained soil in sun or partial shade. Plant in autumn or spring.

▲ *Lamium maculatum*

▼ *Lamium maculatum* 'Aureum'

PROPAGATION
Lift and divide these plants in the autumn or spring.

POPULAR SPECIES
L. maculatum (Europe). Known as the spotted dead-nettle, this has somewhat triangular leaves with an irregular, central, silver-white band; pale red-purple flowers on stems at least 20cm (8in) high; early to late summer. There are several varieties: 'Album', with white flowers; 'Aureum', with bright green-yellow leaves; and 'Roseum', in soft clear pink.

▲ *Lathyrus latifolius*

LATHYRUS
(Sweet pea)

This is an 'old-fashioned', favourite climbing plant, traditionally grown in cottage gardens up the house wall, or at the side of the front door. It produces a long succession of typical sweet-pea flowers. It can, of course, also be grown in herbaceous or mixed borders, given suitable support such as tall twiggy sticks. Or it can be allowed to scramble at will – perhaps on a bank, where it would spread and make good ground cover.

HOW TO GROW

Grow in well-drained, humus-rich soil (add peat or leaf-mould before planting) in a sunny position. Plant in autumn or spring.

PROPAGATION

Divide, or sow seeds, at planting time.

POPULAR SPECIES

L. latifolius (Europe, widely naturalized in USA). Also popularly known as the everlasting pea. Rose-purple or white flowers are produced in abundance in late summer. 3m (10ft) or so.

LIATRIS
(Button snakeroot, blazing star, Kansas gay-feather)

These are clump-forming herbaceous perennials with narrow grassy leaves and bold spikes of flowers that open from the top downwards. They are almost 'essential' plants for herbaceous borders or island beds, flowering in late summer and autumn. Liatris are also a good choice for planting in cottage gardens.

HOW TO GROW

Grow in any well-drained but not dry soil, preferably humus rich (add peat or leaf-mould before planting), in full sun. Plant in autumn or spring.

PROPAGATION

Lift and divide established clumps in the autumn or spring.

▼ *Liatris spicata montana* 'Kobold'

POPULAR SPECIES

L. pycnostachya (C. to S.E. USA). Produces dense spikes of rose-purple flowers in summer and autumn. Up to 1.5m (5ft).
L. spicata (L. callilepis) (S.E. USA). Dense spikes of rose-purple flowers in late summer and autumn. Up to 1.5m (5ft). *L.s. montana* is lower-growing than the species and a well-known variety is 'Kobold'. 60cm (2ft).

LIBERTIA

Evergreen clump-forming perennials with sword-shaped leaves in fan-like clusters, they have erect wiry stems that carry three-petalled flowers followed by yellow or orange-tinted seed pods. These are distinctive plants, which look good in a shrub or mixed border, perhaps with a background of dark green foliage shrubs; they are also suitable for herbaceous beds and borders.

▼ *Libertia formosa*

HOW TO GROW

Libertias need a well-drained but moisture-retentive soil, ideally rich in humus (add peat or leaf-mould before planting). The soil must be acid to neutral because these plants will not tolerate lime. Plant libertias in a position in sun or light shade. Plant in spring.

PROPAGATION

Divide after flowering or in spring.

POPULAR SPECIES

These are all moderately hardy but are damaged in severe frosts and should be protected by covering with dry bracken or straw in winter.
L. formosa (Chile). White flowers, freely produced in early summer. 60–120cm (2–4ft).
L. grandiflora (New Zealand). Pure white flowers, summer. 90cm (3ft).

▲ *Ligularia dentata*

LIGULARIA

These are bold, herbaceous, clump-forming plants with large lower leaves and upright stems carrying showy daisy-like flowers. The ligularias are ideal for moist

Ligularia stenocephala 'The Rocket'

places and can be grown in shrub or mixed borders, on the edge of a woodland garden, in a herbaceous bed or border or near a pond or pool.

HOW TO GROW

Grow in moisture-retentive soil in sun or partial shade. Plant in autumn or spring.

PROPAGATION

Lift and divide at planting time, or sow seeds in the spring.

POPULAR SPECIES

L. dentata (L. clivorum, Senecio clivorum) (China, Japan). Large, round or kidney-shaped leaves; bright orange-yellow flowers in late summer. 90–120cm (3–4ft). 'Desdemona' has rich red-purple stems and leaf undersides and bright orange flowers.
L. przewalskii (Senecio przewalskii) (N. China). Large lobed leaves; black-purple stems; yellow flowers in late summer. 1.5m (5ft).
L. stenocephala (Senecio stenocephala) (China, Japan, Taiwan). Large leaves on deep purple stems; yellow flowers in summer. 1.5–2m (5–6½ft). 'The Rocket' is a good variety.

LIMONIUM
(Sea lavender, statice)

These are clump-forming herbaceous or evergreen perennials which produce upright wiry stems that bear sprays of flowers in the summer. They are highly recommended for herbaceous borders or island beds, and cottage gardens. The flowers are suitable for cutting, and can also be dried for winter arrangements.

HOW TO GROW

Limonium grows in any well-drained soil as long as the position is in full sun. Plant in autumn or spring.

PROPAGATION

Lift and divide clumps in spring, or plant root cuttings in winter.

POPULAR SPECIES

L. latifolium (Statice latifolium) (S.E. Europe to USSR). Evergreen; large sprays of light violet-blue flowers in late summer. 30–45cm (1–1½ft). Varieties include 'Blue Cloud', lavender blue; 'Violetta', violet.

▼ *Limonium latifolium* 'Violetta'

▲ *Linum narbonense*

HOW TO GROW

Grow in well-drained soil in the sun. Plant in spring or autumn.

PROPAGATION

Sow seeds or plant cuttings, in spring.

▼ *Linum perenne alpinum*

LINUM
(Flax)

Popular, tufted, herbaceous perennials for herbaceous borders and beds, they are recommended, too, for planting in cottage gardens. They produce lots of small bowl-shaped flowers in summer and the best-loved colour is blue.

▲ *Linum flavum*

POPULAR SPECIES

L. arboreum (Crete). This shrub-like plant is half-hardy in cold areas but does well in milder regions. Rich yellow flowers, summer. 30cm (12 in).

L. flavum (C. and S.E. Europe). Commonly known as the yellow flax; yellow flowers in summer. 45–60cm (1½–2ft).

L. narbonense (C. and W. Mediterranean to N.E. Portugal). Like a robust *L. perenne*, with azure-blue flowers. 30–60cm (1–2ft).

L. perenne (L. sibiricum) (mainly C. and E. Europe). Blue flowers in summer. 60cm (2ft) high.

LIRIOPE
(Lily turf)

This is a very useful and attractive evergreen perennial, which is valued for its spikes of autumn flowers. It has grassy foliage throughout the year and makes an ideal plant for the front of herbaceous, mixed and shrub borders; it is also recommended for cottage gardens. A beautiful effect can be created if liriope is mass planted around shrubs which have autumn leaf colour and berries.

▲ *Liriope muscari*

▲ *Lobelia cardinalis*

HOW TO GROW

Grow in any well-drained, preferably light sandy soil, acid to neutral. This is a drought-resistant plant so it does not matter if the soil is inclined to dry out in summer. Liriope thrives in sun or partial shade. Plant this perennial in spring.

PROPAGATION

Lift and divide established clumps in spring, or sow seeds when ripe.

POPULAR SPECIES

L. muscari (L. platyphylla, L. graminifolia densiflora) (China, Japan). Dense clump-forming plant with deep green arching leaves; lavender flowers, in dense spikes, produced in autumn. 30–45cm (1–1½ft). The variety 'Majestic' is very robust and has violet flowers.

LOBELIA

Some of these border perennials are half-hardy and need to be overwintered under glass. They are suitable for herbaceous or mixed borders and produce highly colourful tubular flowers in the summer.

HOW TO GROW

Grow in well-drained humus-rich soil (add peat or leaf-mould before planting), in a sunny sheltered position. Provide protection in winter in all but the mildest areas, or keep in a cool greenhouse. Plant in spring.

PROPAGATION

Divide in spring.

POPULAR SPECIES

L. cardinalis (E. USA). Known as the cardinal flower; half-hardy; evergreen, leaves often flushed red-purple; scarlet flowers in late summer. Variety 'Queen Victoria' has beetroot-coloured leaves.

▼ *Lobelia siphilitica*

▲ *Lobelia splendens* 'Jean'

▲ *Lunaria annua*, purple

60–90cm (2–3ft). Overwinter under glass.
L. erinus (S. Africa). Low-growing,
spreading plant; light blue and white flowers,
early summer. 20cm (8in).
L. siphilitica (E. USA). Commonly called the
blue cardinal flower; hardy; bright blue
flowers in late summer and autumn. 60–90cm
(2–3ft).
L. splendens (L. fulgens) (S. USA, Mexico).
Half-hardy; similar to *L. cardinalis*. 60–90cm
(2–3ft). Overwinter under glass.

LUNARIA
(Honesty, satin flower)

This is an 'old-fashioned', well-loved
cottage-garden plant which is classed as
a biennial, although it can be a short-lived
perennial. In any event it sows itself freely
so once planted you should never be without
plants. It is suitable also for shrub and
mixed borders and for the edge of a
woodland garden. The rounded, papery,
silvery seed pods are often dried and used in
winter arrangements.

HOW TO GROW

Grow in any well-drained soil in sun or
shade. Plant in autumn.

PROPAGATION

Sow seeds where plants are to flower, or in
a nursery bed, in late spring to early
summer; transplant if necessary in autumn.

POPULAR SPECIES

L. annua (L. biennis) (S.E. Europe,
naturalized elsewhere). Four-petalled
flowers are produced in spring or early
summer, and come in shades of red-purple
or white. Up to 90cm (3ft). The variety
'Variegata' has leaves edged with creamy
white, and crimson flowers.

LUPINUS
(Lupins)

The lupins are surely among the top ten
favourite herbaceous plants, producing
their bold spikes of scented flowers in early
summer. No self-respecting cottage garden
should be without them, but they look
equally good in modern herbaceous or mixed
borders. Beautiful effects can be created by
grouping lupins with other early summer-
flowering perennials, such as the bearded
hybrid irises, peonies and Oriental poppies.

Lupinus 'Blue Jacket' ▷

perennial with tall spikes of blue, purple or red flowers in early summer. Up to 1.5m (5ft) high. It is mainly represented in gardens by hybrids with the tree lupin, *L. arboreus*, resulting, after many years of breeding and selection work, in the famous Russell strain with flowers in all colours of the rainbow, including bi-coloured blooms. Russell lupins may be raised from seed as complete mixtures or with more restricted colour selections; for example yellow shades, rose and white, blue and white, or obtained as plants of named varieties. They rarely exceed 90cm (3ft) in height. Dwarf lupins are also available, which are suitable for narrow or small borders.

▲ *Lupinus arboreus*

The finger-like foliage of lupins is also quite attractive and provides lush greenery in the spring and summer. The flowers can be used for cutting and arranging.

HOW TO GROW

The best results are obtained in acid (lime-free) or neutral soil. Lupins can be grown in heavy soils, but they are longer-lived in light sandy soils. Make sure the soil is not too rich, otherwise lush vegetative growth will be produced and the flower stems will then probably need the support of canes. Lupins grow equally well in sun or partial shade. Plant in autumn or spring. Cut off dead flower spikes to encourage more blooms to be produced later in the summer.

PROPAGATION

You can divide the plants at planting time, but better results come from soft basal cuttings taken in spring and rooted under glass. Lupins also sprout readily from seeds sown in spring and often flower in their first year. Seedsmen offer packets of mixed hybrids and these are recommended.

POPULAR SPECIES

L. polyphyllus (California to British Columbia). This is a clump-forming

LYCHNIS
(Catchfly)

Clump-forming or tufted herbaceous perennials, these plants make a long and colourful display in herbaceous borders and beds during summer. They are suitable too for mixed borders, and highly recommended for cottage-garden planting schemes. Because they have very strongly coloured flowers, lychnis is ideally grouped with silver- or grey-leaved perennials or shrubs, which make a pleasing foil.

HOW TO GROW

The catchflies are very adaptable and will succeed in any soil which has good drainage. They do, however, appreciate a reasonably fertile soil and a position in full sun is essential. Plant in autumn or spring.

PROPAGATION

Lift and divide established clumps at planting time; or sow seeds in spring and grow the young plants on in a nursery bed until autumn, when they can be planted in their permanent positions.

POPULAR SPECIES

L. × arkwrightii (L. chalcedonica × L. × haageana). A hybrid plant, midway between its parents, with intense scarlet flowers in the summer. 30cm (12in).
L. chalcedonica (N. USSR). The Maltese or

▲ *Lychnis × arkwrightii*

▲ *Lychnis chalcedonica*

▼ *Lychnis coronaria* 'Abbotswood Rose'

▼ *Lychnis flos-jovis*

Jerusalem cross; flat heads of bright scarlet flowers in summer. 90cm (3ft).

L. coronaria (Agrostemma coronaria) (S.E. Europe). Known as the rose campion or dusty miller; a biennial or short-lived perennial which usually flowers in its first year from seed if sown early in year; unusual purple-cerise (or white) flowers in summer and autumn. 60cm (2ft).

L. flos-jovis (Agrostemma flos-jovis) (Alps). Called the flower of Jove, it is a white woolly perennial with red-purple or white flowers in early summer. 60cm (2ft). 'Hort's Variety' has rose-pink flowers.

L. × haageana. A hybrid with bright orange, scarlet or white flowers in summer; short-lived and rather weak stemmed, but striking. 30cm (12in).

Lysimachia clethroides

Lysimachia nummularia

Lysimachia punctata

LYSIMACHIA
(Loosestrife)

These are very easily grown and colourful perennials which have several uses; for instance, in herbaceous borders or beds, or in mixed borders, you could grow the clump-forming kinds such as *L. clethroides* and *L. punctata.* They have an extremely long flowering season and are very worthwhile border plants. Of very different habit is *L. nummularia,* a prostrate creeping perennial which makes marvellous ground cover among shrubs or roses. All the loosestrifes are traditionally grown, too, in cottage gardens, particularly the well-loved *L. nummularia.*

This can also be grown at the edges of containers, if desired, such as window boxes and tubs. Allow it to cascade down the sides. If it is grown in a border or bed, though, try planting some miniature bulbs through it for spring colour, such as snowdrops

(Galanthus), muscari, scillas, chionodoxas and crocuses.

HOW TO GROW

The loosestrifes like a moisture-retentive soil, making rather poor growth if it is prone to drying out in the summer. Therefore before planting add a good quantity of peat or leaf-mould to the soil. The plants can be grown equally well in sun or shade. *L. nummularia*, especially, is excellent for shady places. Plant in autumn or spring.

PROPAGATION

Lift and divide established plants in the autumn or spring.

POPULAR SPECIES

L. clethroides (China, Japan). Called the gooseneck loosestrife, it spreads by rhizomes (underground stems), forming dense colonies; white flowers in dense, tapered, arching spikes in summer and autumn. 90cm (3ft).
L. nummularia (Europe). Known as creeping Jenny or moneywort. This is a prostrate mat-forming plant, the stems attaining up to 60cm (2ft) in length; rounded light green leaves; bright yellow cup-shaped flowers in summer. Variety 'Aurea' has golden-green leaves.
L. punctata (E. C. and S. Europe). A vigorous species which spreads quickly by rhizomes and forms thick colonies; must have adequate space; spikes of yellow starry flowers in summer; 90cm (3ft).

Lythrum virgatum 'The Rocket'

LYTHRUM
(Purple loosestrife)

There are several species of these clump forming herbaceous perennials, but generally only one is grown — the purple loosestrife. It is especially recommended for wet ground or for poolside planting, but will succeed in a herbaceous or mixed border provided the soil does not dry out.

HOW TO GROW

A moisture-retentive soil is needed; growth will be poor in soils which dry out in summer. Add peat or leaf-mould before planting. Grow in sun or shade.

PROPAGATION

Lift and divide established plants at planting time. in autumn or spring.

POPULAR SPECIES

L. salicaria (Europe, N. Africa, W. and N. Asia, naturalized in the USA). Upright habit; long, dense, tapered spikes of rose-purple to magenta flowers in summer. 90–120cm (3–4ft). Several varieties with richer, brighter or pinker flowers are available, some of them probably hybrids with the shorter, more slender *L. virgatum*. The variety 'The Rocket' is popular.

MACLEAYA
(Plume poppy)

These are herbaceous perennials with large, rounded, lobed leaves and branching heads of tiny flowers in late summer. They are impressive plants for shrub or herbaceous borders; indeed, macleaya is so distinctive that it could be used as a specimen plant, say in a lawn. Macleayas spread underground by means of suckers.

HOW TO GROW

Grow in moisture-retentive, fertile soil in sun or light shade. Plant in autumn or spring.

Macleaya microcarpa

PROPAGATION

Take root cuttings in late winter and root them under glass; lift and divide established clumps in spring; take cuttings of non-flowering lower shoots, or lift suckers, and plant in summer.

POPULAR SPECIES

M. microcarpa (Bocconia microcarpa) (C. China). The large lower leaves are white and downy beneath; large heads of tiny buff-pink flowers in late summer. 2.4m (8ft). 'Coral Plume' has coral-pink flowers.

Matteuccia struthiopteris

MATTEUCCIA
(Ostrich fern)

This is a very striking, tall fern for moist places, ideal for including in, say, woodland gardens or mixed borders, used as a 'cool' foil for other plants which like similar conditions, such as the candelabra primulas and meconopsis, or blue poppies.

HOW TO GROW

Grow in moist, humus-rich soil (add plenty of peat or leaf-mould before planting), and in partial shade or sun. Plant in the autumn or spring.

PROPAGATION

Lift and divide established clumps during planting time.

POPULAR SPECIES

M. struthiopteris (Onoclea struthiopteris)
(Europe, Asia). This is a deciduous fern
which spreads by far-creeping rhizomes
(underground stems); it has arching, very
deeply 'cut' fronds forming a vase- or
shuttlecock-shaped rosette. The fronds
attain a length of 60 to 120cm (2–4ft).

MECONOPSIS
(Poppies)

This genus includes the beautiful blue
poppies which, although very exotic-
looking, are not too difficult to grow given
the right conditions. They enjoy cool
woodland and are beautiful companions for
other plants which like similar conditions,
such as the candelabra primulas and ferns.
Such groups can be drifted among
rhododendrons, azaleas and camellias, if you
have an acid or lime-free soil.

Of course, not everyone has the good
fortune to own a woodland garden, but most
people have a shrub border and this is the

next best place to grow the blue poppies.
Also in woodland or a shrub border you
might like to establish carpets of the Welsh
poppy with yellow or orange flowers.

HOW TO GROW

Grow meconopsis in humus-rich soil – add
plenty of peat or leaf-mould before planting.
It should be well-drained. Clay or close-
textured soils should be liberally dressed
with grit and peat or leaf-mould, which are
forked into the top 20cm (8in) or so. The
position should be in partial shade and
protected from strong winds. Plant in spring
or early autumn.

PROPAGATION

Collect and sow seeds as soon as ripe,
germinating them under glass. Perennial
species may be carefully divided, or offsets
removed, in spring.

POPULAR SPECIES

M. betonicifolia (M.baileyi) (China, Tibet,
Upper Burma). This is the blue poppy; wide
poppy flowers, sky-blue on acid soils,

Meconopsis grandis

lavender on alkaline soils, early summer. Tends to be biennial (or die after flowering). 1m (3ft) high.

M. cambrica (W. Europe). Known as the Welsh poppy; tufted perennial; yellow or orange flowers in late spring. 45–60cm (1½–2ft) high.

▼ *Meconopsis cambrica*

M. grandis (Himalaya). Like a superior *M. betonicifolia;* gentian-blue or purple flowers, early summer; usually reliably perennial. One of its hybrids, 'Branklyn', with vivid blue flowers, is also recommended. 60cm (2ft).

M. regia (Nepal). This species dies after flowering, so renew from seeds. Yellow flowers in summer. 1.5m (5ft).

◄ *Meconopsis betonicifolia*

MENTHA
(Mint)

There are several ornamental kinds of mint which have aromatic foliage, like the well-known herb spearmint. They are useful for moist places and wherever foliage interest is needed.

HOW TO GROW
Grow in any moderately fertile, moisture-retentive soil in sun or partial shade. Plant in autumn or spring.

PROPAGATION
Lift and divide at planting time.

POPULAR SPECIES
M. × *gentilis* (Garden hybrid). Ginger or Scotch mint; the variety 'Variegata' is normally grown, with yellow-veined leaves. 30–90cm (1–3ft).

▼ *Mentha* × *gentilis* 'Variegata'

M. suaveolens (M. rotundifolia) (S. W. Europe). Known variously as apple, round-leaved or woolly mint; the variety 'Variegata' (also known as pineapple mint) is grown for decorative purposes; the margins of its leaves are irregularly splashed with creamy white. 45–60cm (1½–2ft).

▼ *Mentha suaveolens* 'Variegata'

▲ *Mertensia virginica*

HOW TO GROW

Grow in well-drained but moisture-retentive soil, rich in humus (add peat or leaf-mould before planting). Plant in sun or light shade. Plant mertensia either in the autumn or in the spring.

PROPAGATION

Divide carefully at planting time, or sow seeds when ripe.

POPULAR SPECIES

M. echioides (Himalaya). Good ground-cover plant. Heads of deep blue tubular flowers in summer. 30cm (12in).
M. virginica (Kansas to New York and Alabama). Popularly called the Virginia cowslip or bluebell; grey-green foliage; pendulous flowers in violet-blue, spring. This plant grows best in the shade of trees. It dies down in summer. 45–60cm (1–1½ft).

MERTENSIA

These are tufted or clump-forming herbaceous perennials with heads of small tubular flowers in spring or summer. They are very attractive when planted in bold groups at the front of a shrub border or on the edge of a woodland garden.

MILIUM
(Millet)

These are tufted, ornamental grasses of which only one perennial kind is generally grown, the beautiful golden wood millet. This is one of the few ornamental grasses that thrive in shade and therefore is ideal for planting in a woodland garden, or for drifting among shrubs at the front of a shrub or mixed border.

HOW TO GROW

Milium should be grown in well-drained yet moisture-retentive soil. It makes poor growth if the soil dries out in the summer. It should preferably be planted in shade. Ideally plant in spring, otherwise plant in early autumn.

▼ *Milium effusum* 'Aureum'

PROPAGATION

Lift and divide established clumps, or sow seeds, in spring.

POPULAR SPECIES

M. effusum 'Aureum' (Europe, Asia, N.E. USA). A tufted perennial with narrow arching leaves up to 30cm (12in) in length. These are a beautiful shade of golden-yellow. This grass flowers in early to late summer, but the flowers are not particularly significant. 60–150cm (2–5ft) when in flower.

MISCANTHUS
(Ornamental grass)

The ornamental miscanthus are bold, clump-forming herbaceous grasses with broad foliage, which can create dramatic effects in a garden, especially if contrasted with other plants. For instance, they can be grown in a gravel area with plants such as yuccas, phormiums, eryngiums and kniphofias. They also associate well with many shrubs, particularly purple-leaved kinds such as varieties of *Cotinus* and *Berberis*. In the herbaceous bed or border

they look good with plants which have strongly coloured flowers, including many of the varieties of *Phlox paniculata.*

The miscanthus also combine well with modern architecture and paving and so are ideally suited to planting in patio beds and borders. Of course, they should be included in any collection of ornamental grasses, which can make an attractive feature in themselves. The miscanthus also made good specimen plants.

HOW TO GROW

Grow in moisture-retentive soil in full sun or partial shade. Plant in autumn or spring.

PROPAGATION

Lift and divide established clumps in the autumn or spring.

▼ *Miscanthus sinensis* 'Zebrinus'

POPULAR SPECIES

M. sacchariflorus (Imperata sacchariflorus) (Asia). Known as the Amur silver grass; spreads vigorously and forms colonies by means of thick rhizomes (underground stems), but does not get out of control; very wide long green leaves. 3m (10ft) or more.
M. sinensis (Eulalia japonica) (Asia). Also

clump-forming, spreading by thick rhizomes; the wide leaves have a green-white mid-rib. 3m (10ft). There are several excellent varieties: *M. s.* 'Gracillimus', a much smaller plant; *M. s.* 'Variegatus', highly recommended for its leaves which have a conspicuous central cream stripe; and *M. s.* 'Zebrinus', probably the best known, and certainly one of the most striking varieties, with leaves horizontally banded with creamy-yellow.

MOLINIA
(Ornamental grass)

These small but attractive ornamental clump-forming herbaceous grasses create a marvellous effect when mass-planted in front of coloured foliage or flowering shrubs. They also look good drifted among shrub roses and are ideal, too, for patio beds and borders and in cottage-garden planting schemes.

HOW TO GROW

Grow in moisture-retentive soil in full sun, although partial shade is tolerated. Plant in spring or early autumn.

▼ *Molina caerulea* 'Variegata'

PROPAGATION

Lift and divide established clumps in spring.

POPULAR SPECIES

M. caerulea (Europe, Asia). Popularly known as the purple moor grass; densely clump-forming; herbaceous; narrow arching green leaves; green-purple flowers in late summer. Flower stems 45–75cm (1½–2½ft). More attractive is the variety 'Variegata' which has creamy-white striped leaves, often tinged with pink when young.

MONARDA
(Bergamot, bee balm, oswego te)

Monardas are very popular, clump-forming, erect, herbaceous perennials with dense heads of tubular flowers in summer and autumn. Often the flowers are very strongly coloured and they are attractive to bees.

These are favourite cottage-garden plants and should be included in every such garden. However, they are almost essential plants for modern herbaceous borders and island beds because they provide colour over an extremely long period. They are also suitable

for mixed borders because they contrast well with shrubs, including shrub roses.

Good companion plants include perennials with spikes of flowers, such as delphiniums. Silver- and grey-leaved perennials can be recommended as well – these provide an excellent foil for the strong colours that are often found among the varieties of monarda. Ornamental variegated grasses make ideal companions, especially *Phalaris arundinacea* 'Picta'.

HOW TO GROW

Grow in any moisture-retentive soil in sun or partial shade. Growth may be poor in soils which dry out in the summer. Plant in autumn or spring.

PROPAGATION

Lift and divide established clumps in the autumn or spring.

POPULAR SPECIES

M. didyma (E. USA). The flowers are bright scarlet and produced in summer and autumn. A vigorous, spreading plant in the right conditions. 60-90cm (2–3ft). There are numerous varieties, and these are generally grown rather than the species. Popular

▼ *Mondarda didyma* 'Cambridge Scarlet'

varieties include 'Adam', with scarlet flowers; 'Cambridge Scarlet', with crimson-scarlet flowers; 'Croftway Pink', which has pink flowers; 'Snow Queen', with white flowers; and 'Violet Queen', with violet-purple flowers.

▼ *Monarda didyma* 'Croftway Pink'

N

NEPETA
(Catmint)

Some of the catmints are popular cottage-garden plants, particularly *N.* × *faassenii* and *N. mussinii.* These are bushy, rather sprawling perennials with grey-green aromatic foliage and blue flowers from summer to autumn. They are traditionally used for edging beds and borders.

In modern gardens catmints make admirable companions for bush and shrub roses, either for edging the beds or as ground cover among the roses. They also look good with pink-flowered perennials, especially *Dianthus* (pinks and border carnations).

Other uses include ground cover on dry sunny banks, and drifting around purple-leaved shrubs, such as varieties of *Cotinus* or *Berberis.*

HOW TO GROW

Catmints are easily grown in any well-drained soil with full sun. Plant in autumn or spring.

PROPAGATION

Lift and divide established clumps, or plant cuttings, in the spring.

POPULAR SPECIES

N. × *faassenii (N. mussinii* × *N. nepetalla).* A bushy perennial with grey downy foliage and spikes of violet-blue flowers from early summer to autumn. This species is often confused with *N. mussinii,* but is a much better garden plant, and with sterile flowers (they do not set seeds). Up to 45cm (1½ft).

N. mussinii (Caucasus, Iran). Bushy but rather prostrate, mat-forming plant. It has grey-green foliage and spikes of lavender-blue flowers from summer to autumn. This plant seeds freely on lighter soils and is sometimes invasive. Up to 30cm (12in) high.

N. nervosa (Kashmir). Also bushy, this perennial has narrow, long green leaves. Its flowers are usually blue, sometimes yellow,

and bloom on dense spikes in summer. 60cm (2ft) high.

N. 'Six Hills Giant'. This hybrid is very similar to a giant *N.* × *faassenii;* 90cm (3ft).

N. 'Souvenir d'André Chaudron' (*N.* 'Blue Beauty'). Probably a hybrid of *Dracocephalum sibiricum* and like a more compact form of it. Tubular lavender-blue flowers in summer. 45cm (1½ft).

▲ *Nepeta* × *faassenii*

▼ *Nepeta* 'Six Hills Giant'

OENOTHERA
(Evening primrose)

These are very showy herbaceous perennials, usually with large cup-shaped yellow flowers. They vary from low prostrate plants to tall upright kinds and all are highly recommended for planting in herbaceous borders and island beds, for a long show of colour in the summer. They are suitable, too, for cottage-garden borders.

Oenothera missouriensis

Oenothera tetragona fraseri

HOW TO GROW

The oenotheras need a well-drained soil in a position which receives plenty of sun. Any marginally hardy sorts should be given a sheltered position. Plant hardy species in the autumn or spring, but all the less hardy types in spring only.

PROPAGATION

Divide hardy clump-forming species in the autumn or spring, or plant cuttings of young shoots in early summer. Hardy and half-hardy species can be raised from seeds in spring.

POPULAR SPECIES

O. acaulis (Chile). Tufted plant, usually short-lived; pure white flowers, becoming pale rose-purple with age, opening late afternoon or evening; not reliably hardy. 15cm (6in).
O. fruticosa (E. USA). Hardy perennial; deep yellow flowers in summer. 30–60cm (1–2ft) high.
O. missouriensis (O. macrocarpa) (Missouri and Kansas to Texas). Low carpeting habit; large bright yellow flowers, often reddening with age, summer to autumn. 15cm (6in).
O. perennis (O. pumila) (E. USA). Erect stems bearing yellow flowers in summer. Up to 60cm (2ft).
O. tetragona (O. fruticosa youngii, O. youngii) (E. USA). Much like *O. fruticosa*. Yellow flowers in summer. 30–90cm (1–3ft). Varieties include: *O. t. fraseri*; 'Fireworks', up to 45cm (1½ft), with waxy-red flower buds; *O. t.* 'Glaber', about 45cm (1½ft), with mahogany-flushed leaves; *O. t.* 'Highlight', which is the same height but has bright yellow flowers. *O. t. riparia*, which forms a low bush about 20cm (8in) tall.

OMPHALODES
(Navelwort)

These little perennials make charming additions to woodland gardens or the front of shrub borders and are valued for their beautiful blue flowers, which are rather like larger versions of forget-me-nots.

▲ *Omphalodes cappadocica* 'Anthea Bloom'

▲ *Ophiopogon jaburan* 'Vittatus'

HOW TO GROW

Grow in moisture-retentive soil well supplied with peat or leaf-mould. They prefer partial or dappled shade. Plant in spring.

PROPAGATION

Lift and divide established plants in spring or after flowering. Or sow seeds under glass as soon as ripe.

POPULAR SPECIES

O. cappadocica (Turkey). Forms colonies by spreading rhizomes (underground stems); deep blue flowers with white eye, early summer. 15–20cm (6–8in). The variety 'Anthea Bloom' has grey-green leaves and sky-blue flowers.
O. verna (C. S. Europe). A mat-forming plant with deep clear blue flowers in spring; best in light shade. The variety 'Alba' has white flowers. 15cm (6in).

OPHIOPOGON
(Lily turf)

These tufted, grassy, evergreen perennials spread by rhizomes or stolons (underground or above-ground creeping stems). The grass-like leaves are rather leathery and the plants have bell-shaped,

nodding flowers followed by berry-like seeds. They are unusual and attractive plants for the front of a mixed, shrub or herbaceous border.

HOW TO GROW

Grow in well-drained, preferably humus-rich, soil in shade. The species described are fairly hardy in all but the severest winters, the tenderest being the variegated forms of *O. jaburan*. Plant in spring.

PROPAGATION

Divide at planting time.

▼ *Ophiopogon planiscapus* 'Nigrescens'

POPULAR SPECIES

O. jaburan (Japan). Lustrous deep green leaves to 60cm (2ft) or more long; white to pale purple flowers, summer. Variety 'Vittatus' has white-striped young leaves which gradually become totally green. 30–45cm (1–1½ft).

O. planiscapus. Usually grown is the variety 'Nigrescens' which has 25cm (10in) long purple-black leaves and grey-white flowers. 15–25cm (6–10in).

ORIGANUM

These are aromatic perennials suitable for rock gardens and screes, for planting in paving and grouping at the front of mixed or herbaceous borders; they are appropriate, too, for cottage gardens.

HOW TO GROW

Grow in well-drained soil in the sun; grow unreliably hardy ones in shelter. Plant them in the spring.

PROPAGATION

Divide at planting time; sow seed or plant cuttings in spring.

POPULAR SPECIES

O. amanum (Turkey). Low bushy plant, 10cm (4in). It has pink flowers which bloom in late summer. This plant needs a sheltered site if it is to flourish.

Origanum dictamnus

O. dictamnus (Greece, Crete). Known as Cretan dittany; this species has white woolly leaves and pink flowers which bloom in summer; unreliably hardy. 20–30cm (8–12in) high.

O. hybridum (Turkey). Similar to *O. dictamnus* but the leaves are smooth and grey-green. The lilac-pink flowers bloom in summer. 25cm (10in).

O. laevigatum (Syria, Turkey). Clumps of grey-green leaves; red-purple flowers in autumn. 30–45cm (1–1½ft).

O. rotundifolium (N. E. Turkey). This species spreads by rhizomes and is clump-forming. It has blue-grey leaves and pale pink flowers which appear in late summer. 10–20cm (4–8in).

OSMUNDA
(Royal fern)

This tall, stately fern is ideal for poolside planting, but it will also grow in moist borders or beds. It is a deciduous clump-forming fern which has attractive fronds, particularly in the autumn when they turn golden-brown. Beautiful companion plants are the astilbes with their pink, red or white plumes of flowers that appear in the summer.

HOW TO GROW

Osmunda needs a moisture-retentive, humus-rich soil (add peat or leaf-mould before planting) and will succeed in sun or partial shade.

PROPAGATION

Lift and divide established clumps in the spring.

POPULAR SPECIES

O. regalis (Europe, W. Asia, India, S. Africa, USA and S. America). Thick rootstock with masses of black roots, often forming a trunk-like base above the soil when grown in wet sites; the pale but bright green fronds, which ripen to an attractive light brown, grow from 1–3m (3–10ft) tall, but normally around 1.2m (4ft) or so under cultivation (see overleaf for illustration).

▲ *Osmunda regalis*

OXALIS

These are dwarf plants suitable for growing on rock gardens and in paving, but the wood sorrel is ideal for naturalizing in woodland gardens. Also grow oxalis at the front of herbaceous or mixed borders.

They have trifoliate or clover-like leaves which close up at night, and small but numerous five-petalled flowers that stud the plants in spring or summer.

HOW TO GROW

Grow in any well-drained soil in sun or partial shade. Plant in autumn or spring.

PROPAGATION

Divide in autumn or spring, or sow seeds in spring.

POPULAR SPECIES

O. acetosella (Europe to Japan). Known as the common wood sorrel; stemless plant spreading by rhizomes; white flowers with lilac veins, spring. 5–10cm (3–4in) tall.
O. adenophylla (Chile, Argentina). A bulbous plant up to 15cm (6in) tall; grey-green leaves; lilac-pink flowers, late spring. Needs warm site.
O. chrysantha (Brazil). Tender, mat-forming plant to 5cm (2in) tall; yellow funnel-shaped flowers, summer; best protected under glass in frosty areas.
O. enneaphylla (S. S. America, including Falkland Islands). Similar to *O. adenophylla;* fragrant, white or pink flowers veined with lavender.
O. laciniata (S. Argentina, Chile). Spreads by scaly rhizomes, forming tufted patches; but otherwise akin to *O. enneaphylla*; up to

Oxalis adenophylla

Oxalis chrysantha

P

PAEONIA
(Peony)

For sumptuous flowers in early summer, and handsome foliage, there are few herbaceous perennials that appeal more than the peonies. Whether they are planted in cottage gardens (as is the tradition) or in modern herbaceous beds and borders, they make a magnificent show, which is even more effective if the plants are grouped with bearded hybrid irises and lupins. Peonies are also excellent companions for shrubs, especially early-summer flowering kinds such as the *Philadelphus*, or mock orange.

The herbaceous peonies are tuberous-rooted and clump-forming, with handsome deeply cut leaves. The large flowers are bowl-shaped to almost flat, and either double or single. The double-flowering species are the most popular.

Paeonia lactiflora 'Mons. Jules Elie'

5cm (2in) tall; flowers fragrant, pink to maroon-purple (usually light purple-blue in cultivation) with darker veins, early summer; hardy, but the soil must be well-drained, especially in the winter.

O. magellanica (temperate S. America). Mat-forming plant up to 5cm (2in) tall; red-tinged leaves; white flowers, summer to autumn; best grown in peaty soil.

HOW TO GROW

Grow in well-drained but moisture-retentive soil, reasonably fertile and high in humus. Add peat, leaf-mould or well-rotted manure before planting. Peonies grow well in sun or shade, but a site which receives early-morning sun, which will scorch the plants, should be avoided. Plant herbaceous peonies in early autumn or spring.

▲ *Paeonia officinalis* 'Rubra Plena'

PROPAGATION

Divide large or congested clumps carefully in spring. Unless you really want to propagate, it is best to leave peonies alone once planted, because they dislike root disturbance and take some time to become established again after lifting. Peonies are very long-lived plants and it is not unusual to come across clumps that were planted 50 or more years ago, and which are still growing and flowering well.

POPULAR SPECIES

P. lactiflora (P. albiflora) (Tibet, Siberia, China). Popularly known as the Chinese peony; the flowers are usually white, sometimes pink or red, and fragrant; they bloom in summer. 60–90cm (2–3ft). Many varieties are listed under this common name and choice is largely a personal matter, but the following can be recommended for garden worthiness: 'Balliol', single, maroon-red; 'Bowl of Beauty', mallow-purple, yellow centre; 'Duchess de Nemours', double, pure white; 'Felix Crousse', double, rose-red; 'Mons. Jules Elie', double, silvery lilac-pink; 'Sarah Bernhardt', rose-purple, edged pink; 'The Moor', single, deep maroon-crimson. *P. officinalis* (France to Albania). This species produces red flowers in early summer. 60cm (2ft). There are many varieties, including 'Alba Plena', double white; 'Anemoniflora', deep pink, crimson and yellow; 'J.C. Weguelin', crimson; 'China Rose', salmon-red flowers with an orange-yellow centre; and 'Rubra Plena', with double, deep red flowers, the old cottage-garden favourite.

PAPAVER
(Poppy)

The most widely grown and best-loved perennial is the oriental poppy, *P. orientale*. In early summer it produces huge bowl-shaped flowers which are often strongly coloured. It combines beautifully with other border perennials such as bearded hybrid irises and lupins.

The only problem with this poppy is that after flowering it looks decidedly tatty for the rest of the summer, and the rough hairy leaves cannot be called attractive by any

▲ *Papaver orientale* 'King George'

means. Therefore, it is the usual practice to plant some other perennial in front of this plant, which will grow up and hide the poppy foliage and produce flowers after it. A perennial about 60cm (2ft) in height should suffice, such as alchemillas, geraniums, oenotheras or potentillas.

Oriental poppies are as much at home in modern herbaceous and mixed borders as they are in traditional cottage gardens.

HOW TO GROW
Grow in any well-drained soil in plenty of sun. Plant in autumn or spring.

PROPAGATION
Divide established clumps in spring, or take root cuttings in early spring and root them under glass.

POPULAR SPECIES
P. orientale (S.W. Asia). A clump-forming herbaceous plant with rough hairy leaves and stems; flowers at least 10cm (4in) wide, red with a black basal blotch to each petal, early summer. 1m (3ft). Varieties are usually grown and some well-tried ones are 'Marcus Perry', orange-scarlet; 'Mrs Perry', clear pink; 'Perry's White', chalk white; 'Salmon Glow', double, salmon-pink.

PELTIPHYLLUM
(Umbrella plant)

This is a bold, large-leaved herbaceous plant generally planted by the side of pools where it flourishes in the moist soil. It will, however, thrive in a border, provided the soil is moist and does not dry out.

▲ *Peltiphyllum peltatum* autumn colour

▼ *Peltiphyllum peltatum* flower heads

HOW TO GROW

The umbrella plant will thrive in any soil as long as it is moisture retentive. It may be placed in either full sun or partial shade. Plant in autumn or spring.

PROPAGATION

Lift and divide established clumps at planting time, or sow seeds in spring and germinate them in a garden frame.

POPULAR SPECIES

P. peltatum (Saxifraga peltatum) (California and Oregon). Herbaceous perennial which spreads by rhizomes (underground stems), forming wide colonies. It has large rounded leaves, up to 25cm (10in) wide, which are boldly lobed, on upright stalks to 1.5m (5ft) or more. The foliage becomes bright red in autumn. Pink or white flowers in large rounded heads, appear on long stems, in spring, before the leaves bud.

PENNISETUM
(Ornamental grass)

These grasses are densely tufted or clump-forming perennials and are unreliable where winters are severe, but in favourable conditions they will persist for several to many years. They are recommended for planting in mixed or herbaceous borders with shrubs and other perennials where they contrast well in shape and texture.

HOW TO GROW

In mild areas, with well-drained soil and a sunny, moderately sheltered position, pennisetums will thrive for a number of years. Plant in spring.

PROPAGATION

Divide in spring; sow seed in spring and grow ideally under glass.

POPULAR SPECIES

P. alopecuroides (E. Asia to E. Australia). Very narrow foliage up to 60cm (2ft) long; yellow, purple or green-white flowers, in

▲ *Pennisetum alopecuroides*

spikes, during summer. 1.5m (5ft).
P. villosum (mountains of N.E. tropical Africa). Feather top; slender arching leaves up to 60cm (2ft) long; stems up to 90cm (3ft), bearing spikes of tawny to white flowers in summer.

PENSTEMON

The border penstemons make a colourful show during summer with their spikes of antirrhinum-like, tubular flowers, but they are not very hardy. They may, however, come through fairly hard winters if grown in very well-drained, dry, sheltered conditions and given additional protection.

HOW TO GROW

The soil must be extremely well-drained. The position should be well sheltered and in full sun. Place cloches over the plants in autumn; remove in spring. Plant in spring.

PROPAGATION

Take cuttings of side shoots in late summer; root under glass. Overwinter young plants under glass. Sow seeds under glass in spring.

POPULAR SPECIES

P. barbatus (Chelone barbatus) (Utah to Mexico). Scarlet flowers with yellow-bearded lip, summer. 'Carnea' is light pink. 1m (3ft) or more.

P. campanulatus (P. pulchellus) (Mexico, Guatemala). Pink, purple or violet flowers. 45–60cm (1½–2ft). Hybrids normally grown, such as the wine-red 'Garnet'.

P. × *gloxinioides.* Varieties of this are grown with flowers in shades of crimson, scarlet, pink and white; in some the flowers are bi-coloured. One variety is 'Pennington Gem', cerise with a white throat. 45–60cm (1½–2ft).

▼ *Penstemon* × 'Pennington Gem'

PEROVSKIA

These shrub-like perennials have aromatic foliage and branching spikes of blue flowers in summer. They contrast beautifully with many other perennials, and with shrubs in mixed borders. They are also recommended for planting in cottage-garden borders.

HOW TO GROW

Grow them in any well-drained soil in sun. Plant in autumn or spring.

PROPAGATION

Take cuttings of non-flowering shoots in summer and plant in a garden frame. Keep under glass over winter.

POPULAR SPECIES

P. atriplicifolia (W. Himalaya, Afghanistan).

▲ *Perovskia atriplicifolia*

White downy foliage; spikes of blue flowers in late summer. Up to 1.2m (4ft). There are several varieties, which are perhaps more widely grown than the species. 'Blue Haze' and 'Blue Spire' are recommended.

PHALARIS
(Gardener's garters; ribbon gras)

These are ornamental grasses and the species normally grown, *P. arundinacea* 'Picta', is an extremely vigorous plant which spreads by rhizomes and forms dense tufts. It is one of the most striking variegated grasses and combines well with strong-coloured perennials, such as many of the

▼ *Phalaris arundinacea* 'Picta'

varieties of border phlox. It is also an excellent companion for shrubs, especially purple-leaved kinds, and shrub roses. Due to its vigorous spread it is not recommended for very small gardens or confined spaces.

HOW TO GROW

Grow in any well-drained soil in sun, although partial shade is tolerated. Plant in autumn or spring.

PROPAGATION

Lift and divide established colonies at planting time. Even very small divisions will soon make large tufts.

POPULAR SPECIES

P. arundinacea 'Picta' (*P. a.* 'Variegata'). Broad arching leaves, 45–60cm (1½–2ft) long, boldly striped with green and white. When mass planted it creates a very light effect. Ideal for stabilizing soil on steep slopes or banks.

PHLOMIS

Most of the phlomis available are strictly shrubs but there are some perennials, which are clump-forming plants with spikes of tubular, lipped, hooded flowers which are quite attractive during the summer. Grow them in herbaceous, mixed or shrub borders. They are particularly good for hot dry places.

HOW TO GROW

Grow in any well-drained soil in full sun. Plant in autumn or spring.

PROPAGATION

Lift and divide established clumps at planting time; raise from seeds sown under glass in the spring.

POPULAR SPECIES

P. russeliana (P. viscosa) (Turkey). This species has leafy stems and long, finely wrinkled, sage-green basal leaves which are hairy underneath; yellow flowers produced in summer. 90–120cm (3–4ft).
P. samia (Greece, S. Yugoslavia). Leafy

▲ *Phlomis russeliana*

stems and long basal leaves, hairy undersides; purple flowers in summer. 1m (3ft) high.

PHLOX
(Border phlox)

The border phloxes are among the top ten herbaceous perennials, loved by nearly all gardeners. They have a long flowering season, from mid- to late summer, and often into early autumn. They are clump-forming, upright plants with large, somewhat rounded heads of five-lobed flowers, in either very strong or more subdued pastel colours. The flowers are quite strongly scented, but the scent is not to everyone's liking because it is rather peppery.

The border phloxes are traditional cottage-garden plants and no self-respecting cottage garden should be without them. However, they are equally at home in modern herbaceous borders or island beds. An excellent companion plant in this situation is the gardener's garters grass, *Phalaris arundinacea* 'Picta', with its green- and white-striped leaves which make a marvellous foil for the strongly coloured species of phloxes.

Phloxes look good, too, in mixed borders, particularly if grown with shrub roses, both old-fashioned and modern varieties. White, pink or red phloxes make excellent companions for purple-leaved shrubs, such as varieties of *Cotinus* and *Berberis*.

▲ *Phlox maculata* 'Omega' foreground

Many people also like to grow the border phloxes for cutting, because the blooms last well in water.

HOW TO GROW

Border phloxes need a moisture-retentive humus-rich soil. If the soil is inclined to dry out during the summer the plants will grow poorly and become stunted. Before planting, especially if the soil is light and sandy, incorporate a good quantity of peat, leaf-mould, garden compost or well-rotted manure. This will help to retain moisture. Although they can be grown in full sun, better results are obtained in partial shade. A mulch of organic matter placed around the plants in spring will help to retain soil moisture further during dry spells. Plant in autumn or spring.

PROPAGATION

Lift and divide established clumps at planting time. Alternatively, propagate from root cuttings in the winter, rooting them in a frost-free greenhouse.

POPULAR SPECIES

P. maculata (E.C. USA). Clump-forming herbaceous plant, often with purple-spotted stems (except in white- or pale-flowered varieties). Fragrant flowers, purple, violet-pink to white, summer. 1m (3ft) or more. Varieties include 'Alpha', with pink flowers; and 'Omega', which has white flowers, tinted with violet.

P. paniculata (P. decussata) (E. USA, from New York south). Clump-forming herbaceous plant with fragrant flowers, rose-purple to white, mid- to late summer through to autumn. 1–1.5m (3–5ft). Varieties are normally grown rather than the species itself, and there are dozens of them. The varieties include 'Bill Green', pink; 'Border Gem', violet-purple; 'Branklyn', dark lilac; 'Eva Cullum', pink; 'Franz Schubert', lilac; 'July Glow', carmine-crimson; 'Prince of Orange', brilliant orange-salmon; 'Red Indian', deep crimson; 'Sandringham', cyclamen pink; 'Starfire', with dark red flowers; 'Vintage Wine', which has purple-red flowers; 'White Admiral', which has pure white flowers; and 'Windsor', with carmine-rose flowers.

PHORMIUM
(New Zealand flax)

The phormiums are clump-forming evergreen perennials from New Zealand and the adjacent islands. They have leathery, sword-shaped leaves and spikes of tubular flowers in summer, but they are essentially foliage plants. The leaves contain tough fibres which are woven to make cloth, mats, baskets, rope, etc.

In recent years the phormiums have become very popular, especially with the introduction of many new varieties with highly coloured foliage. They impart an exotic touch to the garden and perhaps look most at ease in modern settings. For instance, they contrast well with modern architecture and paving and so are ideally suited to planting in patio beds and borders.

Phormium cookianum 'Tricolor'

Phormium tenax

They also make excellent tub plants.

Phormiums can also be recommended for shrub or mixed borders, where they contrast in shape with many shrubs, especially those with palmate (hand-shaped) leaves.

HOW TO GROW

Phormiums like a fertile, moisture-retentive soil, although it should be well drained. A soil which lies wet over winter can cause roots to rot and the plants to die. They are best grown in full sun, although partial shade is tolerated. Phormiums are generally much hardier than often stated in books, but they are liable to damage in severe winters, and in areas of moderate frost are best grown against walls or in other warm sheltered

places. If grown in containers such as tubs, it is a good idea to move these into a frost-free greenhouse for the winter, especially in areas subjected to hard winters because the plants could be killed if the compost and roots remain frozen solid for a prolonged period. Plant in spring.

PROPAGATION

Lift and divide established clumps at planting time, ensuring that each division has several fans of leaves (rather than a single fan), because these help to establish the plant much better.

POPULAR SPECIES

P. cookianum (P. colensoi). Known as the mountain flax; leaves 1–1.5m (3–5ft), sometimes 2m (6ft) long, arching or drooping when mature, usually glossy; flowering stems to 2m (6ft) tall, flowers green to orange or yellow, summer. Several varieties are available, some of hybrid origin with the species *P. tenax.* These include 'Cream Delight', cream- and green-striped leaves; 'Tricolor', leaves striped creamy-yellow and margined red; 'Bronze Baby', leaves bronze, grey-green underneath.
P. tenax. Leaves 1.5–3m (5–10ft) tall, stiff, upright or slightly arching, often grey underneath and bordered with an orange or red line; flowering stems at least 3m (10ft), flowers dull red in summer. Varieties include 'Purpureum' with purple-bronze leaves; 'Variegatum', leaf margins cream; and 'Veitchii', leaves striped cream. Newer varieties include 'Maori Sunrise' with pink, orange and bronze leaves; 'Sundowner', leaves striped grey-purple and cream-pink; and 'Yellow Wave', a low-growing plant with deep yellow and green striped leaves.

PHYSALIS

(Bladder, winter or ground cherry)

The species usually grown, *P. alkekengi,* is a vigorous herbaceous plant which spreads by rhizomes (underground stems). It is at its most colourful in late summer and autumn when it bears bright orange, lantern-shaped seed pods. Give it plenty of space in

▲ *Physalis alkekengi*

a herbaceous or mixed border and combine it with other plants with autumn colours, such as the Michaelmas daisies and shrubs noted for autumn leaf tints or berries.

HOW TO GROW

Grow in any well-drained, moderately fertile soil in sun or partial shade. Plant in autumn or spring.

PROPAGATION

Lift and divide established plants in the autumn or spring.

POPULAR SPECIES

P. alkekengi (P. bunyardii, P. franchetti) (S. E. Europe to Japan). Also popularly known as the Chinese or Japanese lantern; upright stems bearing somewhat triangular leaves and small off-white flowers in summer; bright orange or orange-red lantern-shaped seed pods in late summer and autumn. 45–60cm (1½–2ft).

PHYSOSTEGIA

(False dragonhead, obedient plant)

This is a herbaceous perennial which spreads by rhizomes and forms clumps and colonies. In summer and autumn it makes a colourful show, and it is highly recommended for herbaceous borders and island beds and for cottage-gardens.

HOW TO GROW

Grow in any well-drained soil which does not dry out in the summer. Ideal for full sun or partial shade. Plant in autumn or spring.

PROPAGATION

Lift and divide established clumps at planting time, or take cuttings in spring and root under glass.

POPULAR SPECIES

P. virginiana (including *P. speciosa*) (E. USA, S.E. Canada). Produces spikes of rose-purple flowers in summer and autumn; each flower has a short, hinge-like stalk and will stay put when pushed to the left or right. Up to 1.2m (4ft). Varieties include 'Summer Snow', pure white; 'Summer Spire', rose-pink; *P.v. speciosa* 'Rose Bouquet', soft pink; and *P.v.s.* 'Vivid', deep lilac pink. Varieties are shorter than the species.

▼ *Physostegia virginiana*

PLATYCODON

(Balloon flower)

This is a charming, small, clump-forming herbaceous perennial suitable for the front of herbaceous borders or beds; for large rock gardens and for cottage gardens. The flowers are balloon-shaped in bud, hence the common name, and they expand to a wide bell shape. Platycodon makes a charming show with its blue flowers.

▲ *Platycodon grandiflorus* 'Mariesii'

▲ *Polemonium viscosum*

HOW TO GROW

The balloon flower will succeed in any well-drained, humus-rich soil (add peat or leaf-mould before planting) in a position which receives plenty of sun. Plant in the autumn or spring.

PROPAGATION

Divide plants in the spring, or sow seeds and germinate under glass during that time.

POPULAR SPECIES

P. grandiflorus (E. Asia). This in fact is the only species, a tufted or clump-forming small plant with erect flower stems; the flowers, 5–7.5cm (2–3in) across, are deep to pale purple-blue and appear in summer. 60cm (2ft) or more. Varieties include 'Apoyama' ('Apoyensis'), blue, 15–20cm (6–8in) tall; 'Mariesii', flowers blue and slightly earlier, 45cm (1½ft); 'Mariesii Album', white; 'Mother of Pearl', soft pink; and 'Snowflake', semi-double white.

POLEMONIUM

These attractive herbaceous perennials have fern-like foliage and tubular, lobed flowers in spring or summer. They should be in every cottage garden, and are highly recommended for herbaceous borders and island beds.

HOW TO GROW

Grow in fertile, moisture-retentive but well-drained soil in sun or partial shade. Plant in autumn or spring.

PROPAGATION

Lift and divide established clumps in the autumn or spring.

POPULAR SPECIES

P. caeruleum (N. Hemisphere). Popularly known as Jacob's ladder; blue or white flowers in summer; a very variable species. 60–90cm (2–3ft).

▼ *Polemonium foliosissimum*

▲ *Polemonium caeruleum*

PROPAGATION

Lift and divide established clumps in the autumn or late winter.

POPULAR SPECIES

P. × *hybridum.* A hybrid, and the common Solomon's seal; flowers green-white in summer; 90cm (3ft).
P. multiflorum (Europe to Japan). Much like a less robust *P.* × *hybridum,* flowering in early summer. 60cm (2ft).

▼ *Polygonatum* × *hybridum*

P. foliosissimum (Rocky Mountains south to Arizona). Much like a robust *P. caeruleum,* with deep violet to purple-blue flowers, also white, cream or blue. Remove dead flowers to encourage autumn flowering. 75cm (2½ft).
P. viscosum (P. confertum) (W. USA). Tufted, to 15cm (6in) or more; blue flowers, late spring. Ideal for rock gardens.

POLYGONATUM
(Solomon's seal)

The Solomon's seals are 'aristocratic' yet easily grown woodland plants which flower in the spring. They spread by rhizomes (underground stems) and have upright stems with arching tips, from which dangle rows of white, green-tipped bell-shaped flowers. Failing a woodland garden, grow Solomon's seals in shrub borders, where they will appreciate dappled shade.

HOW TO GROW

Grow in moisture-retentive, preferably humus-rich soil in partial shade, although sun is tolerated. Plant in the autumn or late in winter.

POLYGONUM
(Knotweed)

The herbaceous or evergreen perennial kinds of this plant vary from ground cover to tall bushy plants, all flowering freely over a long period in summer and perhaps into autumn. They are invaluable and easy plants for herbaceous or mixed borders, the shorter ones being ideal, for island beds.

HOW TO GROW

Grow in any moderately rich soil in sun. Plant in autumn or spring.

PROPAGATION

Lift and divide established clumps or mats in the autumn or spring.

Polygonum affine 'Donald Lowndes'

POPULAR SPECIES

P. affine (Himalaya). Mat-forming perennial, the leaves of which become bronze in winter; rosy-red flowers on spikes, autumn. 20–30cm (8–12in). Good varieties are 'Darjeeling Red', with deep crimson flowers; 'Donald Lowndes' ('Lowndes Variety'), with rusty-brown foliage in autumn, and rose-pink flowers.

P. amplexicaule (Himalaya). Clump-forming species with dense, slender spikes of flowers from summer to autumn. 90–120cm (3–4ft). Varieties include 'Atrosanguineum', rich crimson; 'Firetail', similar but brighter shade in large spikes.

P. bistorta (Europe to C. Asia). Known variously as bistort, Easter ledges, snakeroot, snakeweed. Pink flowers on dense spikes, early summer. 45cm (1½ft). Normally grown is the variety 'Superbum', which is larger than the species. Up to 75cm (2½ft).

P. campanulatum (Himalaya). Clump-forming plant with hairy, conspicuously veined leaves; bell-shaped pale pink flowers in summer and autumn. 90cm (3ft).

P. macrophyllum (P. sphaerostachyum) (Himalaya, China). Clump-forming plant akin to *P. bistorta;* spikes of deep rose-red flowers in summer. 45cm (1½ft).

P. milletii (Himalaya to W. China). Akin to *P. bistorta;* dense spikes of deep pink to crimson flowers in summer. 45cm (1½ft).

Polygonum campanulatum

POLYPODIUM
(Common polypody or wall fern)

This is an attractive evergreen fern which spreads by rhizomes, forming mats or colonies. It is an excellent fern for shade, such as beneath trees, but can also be grown on banks and on dry-stone walls.

HOW TO GROW

Grow in well-drained, humus-rich soil in shade. Once established the plants should not be disturbed. Plant in autumn or spring.

PROPAGATION

Divide at planting time (but plants are best left undisturbed).

POPULAR SPECIES

P. vulgare (N. Hemisphere, S. Africa, Kerguelen Islands). The species is normally available; variable in habit, with oval to long fronds, deep green and feathery. Up to 38cm (1ft 3in). There are several popular varieties, including 'Bifidum Cristatum', with crested frond tips; 'Cambricum', broad fronds; 'Cornubiensis', very feathery appearance; 'Longicaudatum'; and 'Pulcherrimum'.

▲ *Polypodium vulgare* 'Pulcherrimum'

POLYSTICHUM
(Shield fern, holly fern)

These are attractive ferns for shady, moist places, such as woodland gardens, shrub borders and cool courtyards. They produce their fronds in rosettes, on thick upright rhizomes or stems.

▼ *Polystichum setiferum* 'Divislobum Densum'

HOW TO GROW
Grow in moisture-retentive but not wet soil, in shade. Plant in autumn or spring.

PROPAGATION
Lift and divide established clumps in spring.

POPULAR SPECIES
P. aculeatum (Europe, Asia and S. America). Popularly called the hard or prickly shield fern; evergreen, deep green, 1m (3ft) long fronds.

P. lonchitis (Arctic and northern temperate zone, mountains farther south). Known as the mountain holly fern; evergreen fronds to 60cm (2ft) long. Needs a cool humid environment.

P. setiferum (P. angulare) (temperate climates, N. and S. Hemisphere). Called the soft shield fern; similar to *P. aculeatum*, but fronds rather soft, arching and drooping, hence its common name. Several varieties, including 'Acutilobum' ('Proliferum'), the plume fern, with fronds bearing numerous tiny plantlets; 'Divisilobum Densum', with very feathery fronds.

POTENTILLA
(Cinquefoil)

The cinquefoils make a highly colourful display during summer in herbaceous or mixed borders or, in the case of dwarf species, on rock gardens. They have single rose-like flowers, not surprisingly perhaps, since they are in the rose family.

HOW TO GROW
Grow in any well-drained, moderately fertile soil in full sun. Plant in autumn or spring.

PROPAGATION
Lift and divide established clumps in the autumn or spring.

POPULAR SPECIES
P. atrosanguinea (Himalaya). Dark velvety red flowers in summer. 45cm (1½ft) or more. This species, plus *P. argyrophylla* and probably *P. nepalensis*, have been hybridized together to create a race of larger flowered,

flowers. *P. a. chrysocraspeda (P. ternata)* has glossy yellow flowers. Ideal for rock gardens and border edging. 15–20cm (6–8in). *P. nitida* (Alps and Appenines). Mat-forming species to 5cm (2in) tall, ideal for rock garden or ground cover; apple-blossom pink flowers, late summer. Good for a limestone scree. *P. tabernaemontani (P. verna)* (Europe to Bylo Russia). Known as the spring cinquefoil; mat-forming, ideal for rock garden or ground cover; yellow flowers in spring and summer. The variety 'Nana' is

▼ *Potentilla nepalensis*

▲ *Potentilla* 'William Rollison'

often double or semi-double varieties, including 'Gibson's Scarlet', bright scarlet; 'Monsieur Rouillard', mahogany-crimson; 'William Rollison', orange-red and yellow; and 'Yellow Queen', bright yellow, red eye. All these make excellent border plants. *P. aurea* (C. and S. Europe). Forms loose mats up to 15cm (6in) tall; golden-yellow

▼ *Potentilla aurea*

smaller and neater than the species.
P. warrenii (P. recta 'Warrenii') (Europe).
Yellow flowers throughout summer. 45cm
(1½ft). Ideal for herbaceous or mixed
borders. Lives for only a few years so must
be replaced regularly.

PRIMULA

This is a huge genus which includes the
primroses and cowslips. The plants are
quite diverse in habit, some being low
rosette-forming plants no more than 15cm
(6in) high, like the primroses; others are tall
plants, up to 1m (3ft), with flowers growing
in tiers around the stems, such as the
candelabra primulas. The candelabra
primulas, especially, are ideal for woodland
gardens, drifted between rhododendrons,
azaleas and camellias. They associate
beautifully with other perennials such as
Meconopsis, ferns and hostas. They are also
suitable for bog and waterside planting near
ponds or pools. The primroses, too, can be
grown on the edge of woodland. Failing
woodland, these kinds of primulas can be
grown effectively in a shrub border, with the
same kind of companion plants.

Some of the smaller primulas such as
P. juliae, are suitable for planting on rock
gardens, or for edging beds and borders.

HOW TO GROW

Most primulas like a cool, moisture-retentive
soil in partial shade. Some prefer very moist
or wet soils and this is indicated where
appropriate in the descriptive list. All like
humus-rich soils so add peat or leaf-mould
before planting. Generally, the best planting
time is spring, or after flowering if the
species blooms in spring.

PROPAGATION

Sow seeds as soon as they are ripe and
germinate them in a garden frame.
Overwinter young plants in the frame and
plant out in spring. Many species can also be
increased by division at planting time.
Primula denticulata can be propagated from
root cuttings in winter under glass.

POPULAR SPECIES

P. aurantiaca (W. China). One of the
candelabra primulas; leaves up to 20cm (8in)
long; flower stems 30cm (12in), bearing
whorls of red-orange flowers in summer.
Suitable for bog or waterside and woodland.
P. beesiana (W. China). Also a candelabra
primula; leaves 20cm (8in) or more long;
flower stems 60cm (2ft), bearing whorls of
rose-carmine, yellow-eyed flowers in
summer. Excellent for bog, waterside or
woodland.
P. bulleyana (W. China). A candelabra
primula; leaves up to 30cm (12in) long;
flower stems to 60cm (2ft) or more tall,
bearing whorls of orange-yellow flowers in
summer. Excellent for bog, waterside or
woodland garden.
P. denticulata (Himalaya). Known as the
drumstick primrose; leaves to 30cm (12in)
long; flower stems up to 30cm (12in) tall,
bearing dense globular heads of lilac to red
or blue-purple flowers between early spring
and early summer. White also available.
Excellent species, very easily grown, and
suitable for drifting among shrubs in the
shrub or mixed border.
P. florindae (S.E. Tibet). This is the giant
cowslip; leaves up to 20cm (8in) long with
red stalks; flower stems up to 1m (3ft) or
more, bearing bright yellow pendulous
fragrant flowers in summer and autumn. For
bog, waterside or woodland (likes very
moist, but not waterlogged, soil).
P. helodoxa (W. China, Burma). A
candelabra primula; leaves up to 35cm (1ft
2in) long; flower stems 90cm (3ft) tall,
carrying bright rich yellow, fragrant flowers
in whorls during summer. For bog, waterside
or woodland.
P. japonica (Japan). A candelabra primula;
leaves to 30cm (12in) long; flower stems to
60cm (2ft) or more tall, carrying whorls of
red-purple flowers in summer. Variable in
colour, several varieties being available,
including 'Miller's Crimson' and 'Postford
White'. Ideal primula for woodland gardens
or shrub borders.
P. juliae (Caucasus). Forms mat-like
colonies, studded with primrose-like bright
purple flowers in spring. 7.5cm (3in). Ideal
for rock gardens.

Primula denticulata 'Alba'

Primula helodoxa

Primula pulverulenta

P. × *pruhoniciana (P.* × *juliana)*. A varied group of primrose-like varieties, generally with flowers in shades of purple or red. Best-known are 'Garryarde Guinevere', leaves flushed bronze-purple, pink flowers on 15cm (6in) stems; and 'Wanda', like a dwarf primrose with claret-crimson flowers. They flower in spring and are recommended for rock gardens and the front of mixed beds and borders.

P. pulverulenta (W. China). A candelabra primula; leaves to 30cm (12in) long; flower stems to 90cm (3ft) tall, covered in white 'bloom', with whorls of dark red flowers in summer. 'Bartley Strain' has flowers in shades of pink. Ideal for woodland gardens or poolsides.

P. rosea (N.W. Himalaya). A dwarf tufted plant, no more than 15cm (6in) high; bright pink, yellow-eyed flowers in spring. The variety 'Grandiflora' has larger flowers than the species. Needs a very moist soil; ideal for bog gardens.

P. secundiflora (W. China). Leaves up to 30cm (12in) long, covered with yellow powder when young; flower stems to 60cm (2ft) tall, bearing funnel-shaped, pendulous, crimson-rose to purple-red, slightly fragrant flowers in summer. Ideal for woodland gardens and shrub borders.

P. sieboldii (Japan). A small tufted primula suitable for rock gardens, up to 20cm (8in) high; pink, purple or white flowers in late spring and summer. Many varieties have arisen in Japan, with often larger, sometimes fringed flowers.

P. sikkimensis (P. microdonta) (Himalaya). Called the Himalayan cowslip; leaves to 30cm (12in) or more long; flower stems to 60cm (2ft) tall, sometimes more; funnel-shaped, pendulous, yellow flowers in early summer. Ideal for drifting in woodland gardens or shrub borders.

P. veris (Europe, W. Asia). This is the cowslip, a well-loved plant. From rosettes of foliage it produces stems up to 30cm (12in) tall bearing deep yellow, nodding, tubular flowers, well scented, in spring. It is a native of chalky meadowland and is ideal for growing in long-grass areas or wild-flower meadows. Suitable, too, for mass planting in shrub borders.

P. vialii (P. littoniana) (W. China). Leaves up to 30cm (12in) long; flower stems up to 60cm (2ft) tall, carrying dense spikes of blue-violet flowers from scarlet buds in summer. The blooms are fragrant. Probably the most distinctive of all primulas. Can be grown in woodland gardens, shrub borders or on rock gardens.

P. vulgaris (P. acaulis) (Europe, W, Asia). This is the common or English primrose, a well-loved dwarf rosette-forming plant bearing large pale yellow fragrant blooms in spring. Will even start to flower in winter if the weather is mild. *P.v. sibthorpii* (Balkan Peninsula, naturalized elsewhere), has pink, red or purple flowers. Several double-flowered varieties of this and ordinary *P. vulgaris* have arisen, the following usually being available: 'Alba Plena', white; 'Lilacina Plena', lavender. There are also several strains of multicoloured, large-flowered primroses, derived from this and various other species.

for rock gardens or for planting at the front of herbaceous or mixed borders but their growth area needs to be restricted because they can become invasive.

HOW TO GROW

Grow in moisture-retentive, moderately fertile soil in partial shade or sun. Plant in autumn or spring.

PROPAGATION

Divide at planting time.

POPULAR SPECIES

P. grandiflora (Europe). Deep violet flowers in summer. About 30cm (12in) tall when in flower. Varieties 'Alba' and 'Rosea' have white and pink flowers respectively. *P.g. webbiana (P. webbiana)* has several varieties. The following are sometimes listed under *P. grandiflora:* 'Loveliness', pale violet; 'Pink Loveliness', clear pink; 'White Loveliness', flowers large, white.

PRUNELLA
(Self-heal)

These evergreen perennials form low, wide-spreading clumps of foliage and upright stems which bear whorled spikes of tubular flowers in summer. They are useful

▽ *Prunella grandiflora* 'Pink Loveliness'

PULMONARIA
(Lungwort)

These popular spring-flowering perennials spread by thick rhizomes (underground stems), forming wide clumps or colonies, and produce funnel-shaped, lobed flowers, usually in shades of blue. They are excellent for mass-planting among shrubs, for the front of herbaceous beds and borders, and are suitable, too, for the edge of woodland gardens.

HOW TO GROW

Grow in moisture-retentive, humus-rich soil in partial shade, although full sun is tolerated, particularly by *P. angustifolia.* Plant in autumn or spring.

PROPAGATION

Divide at planting time.

POPULAR SPECIES

P. angustifolia (P. azurea) (Europe). Known as the blue cowslip; bright blue flowers in spring. 'Munstead Blue' is intense blue. 20–30cm (8–12in).

▲ *Pulmonaria angustifolia*

▼ *Pulmonaria saccharata*

P. officinalis (P. maculata) (Europe). Called the Jerusalem cowslip or sage; white-spotted leaves; red- to blue-violet flowers, spring. 20–30cm (8–12in).
P. rubra (Europe). Brick-red flowers, spring. 20cm (8in).
P. saccharata (Europe). This is the Bethlehem sage; the leaves are conspicuously spotted with white and are quite bristly; flowers are pink, then turn to violet and blue. 30cm (12in) or more. There

are a number of varieties, including 'Argentea', leaves almost entirely silvery-white, possibly of hybrid origin; 'Cambridge Blue', pink and blue; 'Pink Dawn', pink; and 'White Wings', white.

PULSATILLA
(Pasque flower)

This tufted perennial has attractive fern-like foliage and, in the spring, large cup-shaped flowers. It is a dwarf plant, ideal for planting on rock gardens and at the front of herbaceous or mixed borders. It looks good with dwarf spring-flowering bulbs.

HOW TO GROW
The pasque flower needs a well-drained, fertile soil in full sun. Plant in spring or early autumn.

PROPAGATION
Best raised from seeds sown as soon as ripe, in a garden frame. Overwinter young plants in the frame.

POPULAR SPECIES
P. alpina (mountains in W. and C. Europe). Downy flower buds tinted with red and blue open to become white flowers, in summer. 30cm (12in).

▼ *Pulsatilla vulgaris* 'Alba'

△ *Pulsatilla alpina apiifolia*

▽ *Pulsatilla vulgaris* 'Rubra'

PYRETHRUM

The pyrethrums are herbaceous clump-forming perennials which produce large daisy-like flowers in early summer. They are invaluable for herbaceous or mixed borders, combining well with bearded hybrid irises, and the flowers are excellent for cutting.

HOW TO GROW
Grow in well-drained but moisture-retentive, humus-rich soil in full sun. Plant in spring.

PROPAGATION
Lift and divide established clumps during the spring.

POPULAR SPECIES
P. roseum (now *Chrysanthemum coccineum*) (S.W. Asia). The genus is now generally included with *Chrysanthemum*, but the one familiar species is retained here for convenience. It has rather fern-like foliage and 7.5cm (3in) wide daisy-like flowers in early summer, in shades of pink or red. There are numerous varieties, such as 'Avalanche', pure white; 'Brenda', bright cerise; 'Bressingham Red', deep red; 'Eileen May Robinson', salmon-pink; 'Evenglow', salmon-red; 'Kelway's Glorious', rich scarlet; 'Madeleine', double pale pink.

▽ *Pyrethrum roseum* 'Brenda'

P. vernalis (mountains, Europe). Low-growing, tuft-forming species. Cup-shaped white flowers. 15cm (6in).
P. vulgaris (Europe, eastwards to Ukraine). Attractive fern-like foliage, silky when young; flowers up to 7.5cm (3in) wide, cup-shaped, on 20cm (8in) tall stems, pale to deep purple, in spring. Several named forms are available: 'Alba', white; 'Grandis', larger flowers, deep purple-violet, 30cm (12in) tall; and 'Rubra', shades of maroon-red.

121

R

RANUNCULUS
(Buttercup)

Ranunculus, often with typical buttercup flowers, are excellent border plants, providing colour from early summer onwards. The Turban ranunculus are possibly the most colourful, with their large, globular, double flowers which last well when cut and arranged in water.

HOW TO GROW

Grow in any ordinary well-drained soil in full sun. Plant in spring.

PROPAGATION

Lift and divide established clumps during the spring.

POPULAR SPECIES

R. aconitifolius (Europe, C. Spain to C. Yugoslavia). Known as Fair maids of France, fair maids of Kent; clump-forming perennial with lobed leaves and pure white flowers in early summer. 45cm (1½ft). Variety 'Flore Pleno', called white bachelor's buttons, has double flowers.
R. acris (Europe, Asia). Called the common buttercup; it is represented in gardens by

▼ *Ranunculus asiaticus*

the variety 'Flore Pleno', known as bachelor's buttons, with double yellow flowers in early summer. 60cm (2ft).
R. asiaticus (S.W. Asia, Crete). This is the Persian buttercup; tufted to clump-forming tuberous perennial; white, red, yellow or purple flowers in summer. 30–45cm (1–1½ft). Mainly grown are the double-flowered forms, often listed as Turban ranunculus. Tuberous rooted. May survive mild winters in the garden, but tubers are best lifted in autumn and stored dry for the winter indoors.
R. bulbosus (Europe, Asia, N. Africa). The species itself is not grown, but rather its variety 'Pleniflorus' (or 'Flore Pleno'), with double yellow flowers in early summer. 30cm (12in).
R. gramineus (S. Europe). Known as the grass-leaved buttercup; a clump-forming plant with grassy, grey-green foliage; bright yellow, typical buttercup flowers in late spring and early summer. 30–45cm (1–1½ft).

RHEUM
(Rhubarb)

These bold herbaceous perennials grow from thick fleshy roots and form clumps. They have very large attractive leaves and, in summer, bold spikes of flowers. They make excellent specimen plants in lawns, or can be grown with shrubs in mixed borders.

HOW TO GROW

Grow in humus-rich, moisture-retentive soil in sun or partial shade. Plant in the autumn or the spring.

PROPAGATION

Lift and divide established clumps in the autumn or spring.

POPULAR SPECIES

R. alexandrae (Himalaya). Basal leaves to 30cm (12in) long; spikes of flowers in early summer, with conspicuous cream-coloured bracts (modified leaves). 60–120cm (2–4ft).
R. palmatum (N.E. Asia). Large, rounded, lobed basal leaves; red flowers in early summer. 2m (6ft). More attractive are the

varieties 'Atrosanguineum' and 'Bowles Crimson', with leaves more deeply lobed, which are bright red when young, and cerise-red flowers. *R.p. tanguticum* has less deeply lobed leaves, which are usually flushed with purple hues.

▲ *Rheum alexandrae*

▼ *Rheum palmatum*

RODGERSIA

These herbaceous perennials are grown mainly for their large, bold foliage. They can be grown in mixed borders, where they contrast well with many shrubs, in herbaceous beds or borders, where they look good with astilbes, and in patio beds and borders, where they contrast well with paving and with perennials with sword-like leaves. They are clump-forming and spread by rhizomes, and have long-stalked, generally pinnate leaves and spikes of feathery flowers in the summer.

HOW TO GROW

Grow in humus-rich, moisture-retentive soil, in sun or partial shade, on a sheltered site. Plant in autumn or spring.

PROPAGATION

Divide at planting time.

▼ *Rodgersia aesculifolia*

▲ *Rodgersia podophylla*

POPULAR SPECIES

R. aesculifolia (China). Finger-like leaves; white flowers in pyramid-shaped heads, summer. 1–2m (3–6ft).
R. pinnata (China). Pinnate or compound leaves, and rounded clusters of red and white flowers. 1–1.2m (3–4ft). 'Superba' is taller than the species and has bronze-flushed leaves and pink flowers.
R. podophylla (China, Japan). Finger-like leaves; large arching or nodding heads of cream flowers in summer. 1–1.5m (3–5ft).
R. tabularis (N. China, Korea). Large rounded leaves up to 60cm (2ft) wide, with many tooth-like lobes; heads of white astilbe-like flowers in summer. 1m (3ft).

RUDBECKIA
(Coneflower)

The rudbeckias are almost essential plants for herbaceous borders or island beds, producing showy daisy-like flowers over a long period in summer. Each flower has a cone-shaped centre, hence the popular name. They associate well with plants which have spikes of flowers, such as delphiniums and red-hot pokers. The blooms are excellent for cutting and arranging in water.

HOW TO GROW
The coneflowers succeed in any moderately fertile, well-drained soil in full sun or partial shade. Plant in autumn or spring.

PROPAGATION
Lift and divide established clumps in the autumn or spring.

POPULAR SPECIES
R. fulgida (E. USA). Clump-forming plant with bright yellow flowers, purple-brown cone-shaped centre; summer and autumn. 60cm (2ft) or more. *R.f. deamii (R. deamii), R.f. speciosa (R. newmannii, R. speciosa)* and *R.f. sullivantii (R. sullivantii)* are good varieties. The latter is the most frequently grown variety, 'Goldsturm' being an improved selection from it.
R. laciniata (N. USA). Clump-forming perennial with fern-like foliage; yellow flowers, olive-green cone-shaped centre, late summer. 2–3m (6–10ft). 'Soleil d'Or' is similar, and 'Hortensia' ('Golden Glow'), has double, bright yellow flowers.
R. nitida (S.E. USA). Similar to *R. laciniata,* but rarely above 1.2m (4ft) tall, with simple oval or lanceolate leaves. A well-known variety is 'Goldquelle' (often catalogued as *R. laciniata* 'Goldquelle'), with double, brassy yellow flowers.

▲ *Rudbeckia f. sullivantii* 'Goldsturm'

▽ *Rudbeckia nitida* 'Goldquelle'

S

SALVIA

The perennial salvias are excellent summer-flowering plants for herbaceous borders or island beds, especially *S.* × *superba* and its varieties, the flower spikes of which contrast superbly with daisy-flowered perennials. Other species are short-lived or tender perennials but well worth growing.

HOW TO GROW

The soil must be very well drained and

Salvia × *superba*

reasonably fertile. Choose a position in full sun, and make sure it is well sheltered if the plants are on the tender side. The best planting time is spring.

PROPAGATION

Divide at planting time, or sow seeds in spring and germinate under glass.

POPULAR SPECIES

S. haematodes (Greece). This is a short-lived perennial which should be renewed frequently from seed. The leaves are hairy underneath; the blue-violet flowers are carried in large pyramid-shaped clusters during summer. 90cm (3ft) or more. An especially good variety is 'Indigo', derived

from a cross with *S.* × *superba*, with deep blue flowers.

S. patens (mountains of Mexico). This is a short-lived perennial and is suitable for growing outdoors all the year round only in very mild parts of the country because it is tender. It is tuberous-rooted, with hairy leaves; the flowers are gentian-blue and produced in summer. 60–90cm (2–3ft). Best to protect the crowns of the plants in winter by covering with bracken or a cloche.

S. × *superba* (*S. virgata nemorosa).* This is a very popular herbaceous perennial which should be in every border. Throughout summer and into autumn it produces spikes of violet-purple flowers, each surrounded by red-purple bracts (modified leaves). 90cm (3ft) or more. There are some excellent varieties of this, including 'East Friesland', violet-purple, 45cm (1½ft); and 'Rose Queen', rose-pink, 75cm (2½ft).

SANGUINARIA
(Bloodroot, red puccoon)

This is a rather unusual perennial in that all parts of the plant, in particular the roots, exude a red sap when damaged. It is, however, a most attractive plant for cool, shaded spots, perhaps in woodland gardens or in part of a shrub border.

HOW TO GROW
The bloodroot needs a humus-rich,

▼ *Sanguinaria canadensis* 'Multiplex'

moisture-retentive soil, so add plenty of peat or leaf-mould before planting. It also relishes dappled or partial shade, such as that cast by trees. Plant in autumn, or immediately after flowering.

PROPAGATION
Lift and divide established plants during the autumn or after flowering.

POPULAR SPECIES
S. canadensis (E. USA). This is the only species. It spreads by thick fleshy rhizomes and produces rounded, lobed, blue-grey leaves; the white flowers appear in spring with the unfurling young leaves. More attractive is the double-flowered variety 'Multiplex' ('Plena', 'Flore Plena'). 15cm (6in) high.

SANGUISORBA
(Burnet, blood root)

These are clump-forming herbaceous perennials with quite attractive fern-like foliage and globular or cylindrical spikes of brush-like flowers in summer. They are useful for herbaceous borders or island beds.

HOW TO GROW
Grow in fertile, well-drained but not dry soil in a sunny position. Plant in autumn or spring.

▼ *Sanguisorba obtusa*

PROPAGATION

Lift and divide established clumps at planting time.

POPULAR SPECIES

S. canadensis (E. USA). White flowers, in spikes up to 20cm (8in) long. 1.2–2m (4–6ft). *S. minor (Poterium sanguisorba)* (Europe, Asia). This is the salad burnet; green, purple-tinted flowers in globular spikes. 45–60cm (1½–2ft). *S. obtusa* (Japan). Rose-purple flowers. 1.2m (4ft).

▲ *Saponaria ocymoides*

SAPONARIA

These are small perennials ideal for planting at the front of beds and borders, or on rock gardens. They are usually mat-forming plants, studding themselves with masses of small starry flowers in summer.

HOW TO GROW

Grow in any moderately fertile soil in sun. Plant in autumn or spring.

PROPAGATION

Divide at planting time; take cuttings of non-flowering stems and root in late spring or late summer.

POPULAR SPECIES

S. × 'Bressingham Hybrid'. Forms a small flat mat; flowers rich pink; 3.75cm (1½in). *S. ocymoides* (S.W. and S.C. Europe). Mat-forming to 15cm (6in) tall; rose-purple

flowers. There are several varieties: 'Alba', white; 'Rubra', deep red; 'Rubra Compacta', smaller and more compact habit; 'Splendens', deep rose-purple. *S. officinalis* (Europe, Asia, naturalized USA). Popularly known as soapwort. Spreads by rhizomes and forms colonies to 90cm (3ft) tall; pink or white flowers, including double forms. Invasive, best for wild gardens.

SAXIFRAGA

Most of the saxifrages are alpines and normally grown on rock gardens. There are a few, however, which have other uses, particularly London pride, the favourite old cottage-garden plant which is used for edging borders. Unlike most other saxifrages it will grow and flower well in shade. A charming saxifrage for woodland gardens or shrub borders is *S. fortunei*, which also thrives in shade. For the wild-flower meadow or long-grass area *S. granulata*, or meadow saxifrage, is ideal.

HOW TO GROW

The saxifrages described here prefer a moisture-retentive soil of any type. It should be rich in humus, such as peat or leaf-mould. Best in shade or partial shade, except for *S. granulata* which likes a sunny position. Plant in autumn or spring (spring is best for *S. fortunei*).

▼ *Saxifraga fortunei*

PROPAGATION

Lift and divide established clumps in the autumn or spring.

POPULAR SPECIES

S. fortunei (China, Japan). Small clump-forming herbaceous plant with round to kidney-shaped lobed leaves, somewhat fleshy, often purple underneath; dainty, feathery heads of white flowers in autumn. 'Wada's Form' has leaves flushed deep wine-purple. 30–45cm (1–1½ft).
S. granulata (France, Europe). Meadow saxifrage, fair maids of France; tufted to clump-forming herbaceous plant; kidney-shaped leaves; pure white flowers, cup-shaped, appear in spring. 'Flore Pleno' ('Plena') has larger, fully double flowers. 20–30cm (8–12in). In mid-summer the foliage dies down; the plant rests as a cluster of small bulbils just below soil level – these afford an easy means of propagation.
S. umbrosa (W. and C. Pyrenees). London pride; low hummock- or mat-forming plant with deep green, leathery, evergreen foliage; clouds of tiny white flowers, with red dots, appear on 30–45cm (1–1½ft) high stems in early summer. The species itself is uncommon in cultivation; the familiar London pride is *S.* × *urbium. S.u.* 'Primuloides' is a miniature plant with stems to 15cm (6in) tall and pink petals; *S.u.* 'Variegata' has very attractive cream-blotched leaves. *S.* × *urbium (S. spathularis* × *S. umbrosa)* is more rigorous than its parents and it will grow in sites that never receive direct sunlight.

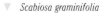

△ *Scabiosa caucasia* 'Clive Greaves'

▽ *Scabiosa graminifolia*

SCABIOSA

(Scabious, pincushion flower)

These clump-forming perennials are excellent long-flowering subjects for herbaceous and mixed borders, producing cushion-like flower heads in summer, which are good for cutting. They are highly recommended, too, for cottage gardens.

HOW TO GROW

Grow in well-drained, moderately fertile soil in sun. Plant in autumn or spring.

PROPAGATION

Lift and divide established clumps in the autumn or spring.

POPULAR SPECIES

S. caucasica (N. Iran, Caucasus, C. and N. Russia). Grey-green, divided upper leaves; heads of lavender-blue flowers early to late summer. 45–75cm (1½–2½ft). There are several very good varieties, including 'Bressingham White', pure white; 'Clive Greaves', rich lavender, one of the most popular varieties; 'Loddon White', creamy white; 'Moerheim Blue', deep lavender-blue.
S. columbaria (Europe, W. Asia, Siberia, N. Africa). This is the small scabious; tufted perennial; fern-like upper leaves; lavender

to lilac flowers summer to autumn. 15–75cm (6–30in). Dwarf forms are mainly grown, up to 15cm (6in) tall, under the names *S. alpina* and *S.a.* 'Nana'.

S. graminifolia (S. Europe). Tufted, usually short-lived perennial; grey-green pinnate or fern-like foliage; mauve to pink flowers in summer. 30cm (12in) or more. Variety 'Pinkushion' has clear pink flowers.

S. ochroleuca (E.C. and S.E. Europe). Almost identical with *S. columbaria* but with pale yellow flowers.

SCHIZOSTYLIS
(Kaffir lily, crimson flag)

These invaluable late-flowering evergreen perennials are highly recommended for warm sheltered places in shrub or mixed borders, combined with other autumn perennials and with shrubs noted for autumn leaf colour and berries.

HOW TO GROW

This plant needs an extremely well-drained yet humus-rich soil in a warm sunny spot. Hardy in sheltered sites, otherwise best protected in winter. Plant in spring.

PROPAGATION

Lift and divide established groups during the spring.

Schizostylis coccinea 'Major'

POPULAR SPECIES

S. coccinea (S. Africa). Clump- or colony-forming perennial which spreads by rhizomes (underground stems); tufts of grassy foliage, evergreen; somewhat crocus-like flowers on stems up to 60cm (2ft) tall, crimson, autumn to early winter. Varieties include 'Gigantea' ('Grandiflora') and 'Major', with flowers larger than those of the species; 'Mrs Hegarty', clear pink flowers; and 'Rosalie' in salmon-pink.

SEDUM
(Stonecrop)

This is a very large group of plants, many of them being dwarf alpine kinds, suitable for rock gardens. However, the border kinds are described here, being suitable for herbaceous borders and beds, and for mixed borders and cottage gardens. One of them, *S. spectabile,* attracts butterflies and is therefore a very popular border plant. They are all succulent plants with fleshy leaves which are rather brittle and easily damaged.

HOW TO GROW

The stonecrops will grow well in any soil, provided it is well drained. The position should be in full sun, as they are great sun-lovers. Plant in autumn or spring.

PROPAGATION

Lift and divide established clumps in the autumn or spring.

POPULAR SPECIES

S. aizoon (Siberia, China, Japan). This is a very colourful, tufted or clump-forming herbaceous perennial with upright stems; it has long leaves with toothed edges; compact clusters of yellow to orange flowers are produced over a long period in summer. 30cm (1ft).

S. rosea (S. rhodiola, Rhodiola rosea) (circumpolar and mountains farther south). This is popularly known as roseroot; it is a herbaceous plant with a very thick and branching rootstock, which is partially above ground. The dried roots are fragrant, hence

▲ *Sedum rosea*

▲ *Sedum spectabile* 'Autumn Joy'

the common name. The long to oval leaves are grey-green; flowers are yellow or green-yellow in compact clusters and are produced from late spring to summer. The foliage contrasts beautifully with the flowers – it is altogether a very eye-catching and attractive plant. 15–30cm (6–12in).

S. spectabile (China, Korea, long cultivated in Japan). In Britain this is known as the ice-plant. It is a clump-forming herbaceous plant with erect stems; the somewhat oval leaves are bright pale grey-green and quite attractive; the pink flowers are carried in flattened heads 10–15cm (4–6in) wide and are produced in late summer and early autumn, lasting for many weeks. The flowers are highly attractive to butterflies. 30–45cm (1–1½ft). There are several varieties, including the well-known 'Autumn Joy', 60cm (2ft) tall, salmon-pink; 'Brilliant', 30cm (12in) tall, deep rose pink; 'Iceberg', 30cm (12in) tall, white; and 'September Ruby', 30cm (12in) tall, dark rose-pink.

S. telephium (Europe, Asia, represented in the USA by the similar *S. telephoides)*. Popularly known as live-forever, live-long, or orpine. A herbaceous clump-forming plant with somewhat oval, toothed, grey-green leaves; purple-red flowers on flat heads are produced in late summer. 60cm (2ft). It is a variable species, including *S.t. maximum (S.*

maximum), more robust, up to 75cm (2½ft) tall, with green- to yellow-white flowers. *S.t.m.* 'Atropurpureum' has dark red-purple leaves and pink flowers – a very attractive and desirable variety. The leaves of *S. t.* 'Variegatum' have cream markings.

SIDALCEA

These very showy border perennials flower in the summer, and should be in every herbaceous or mixed border, and in cottage gardens, too.

▼ *Sidalcea malviflora* 'William Smith'

HOW TO GROW

Sidalceas need moisture-retentive yet well-drained soil. Growth is poor if the soil is prone to drying out in summer. It should also be reasonably fertile. A position in full sun is needed. Plant in autumn or spring.

PROPAGATION

Lift and divide established clumps in the autumn or spring.

POPULAR SPECIES

S. malviflora (S. malvaeflora) (Oregon, California and adjacent Mexico). A clump-forming perennial; the large pink flowers are widely funnel-shaped and carried in clustered heads. 90–120cm (3–4ft). Varieties are usually grown, such as the deep red 'Croftway Red', 1m (3ft) tall; shell-pink 'Loveliness', 75cm (2½ft) tall; large, clear pink 'Sussex Beauty', 1m (3ft) tall; and large, salmon-red 'William Smith', 1m (3ft) tall.

SISYRINCHIUM

These tufted or clump-forming perennials have grassy or sword-shaped leaves and starry or bell-shaped flowers on upright stems. The flowers last a day only but they are produced in succession. They are charming plants for herbaceous borders and island beds, and for mixed borders.

HOW TO GROW

Grow in moisture-retentive but well-drained, preferably moderately fertile soil in full sun. Plant in autumn or spring.

PROPAGATION

Divide at planting time.

POPULAR SPECIES

S. angustifolium (S. gramineum) (USA). Known as blue-eyed grass; blue flowers, summer. 30–45cm (1–1½ft).
S. bermudiana (S. iridioides) (Bermuda). Violet-blue flowers with yellow eye, summer. 30cm (12in).
S. californicum (California to Vancouver Is.). Called golden-eyed grass; bright yellow flowers, summer. 15–60cm (6–24in).

Sisyrinchium striatum

S. striatum (S. Chile). Iris-like, sword-shaped leaves; long spikes of pale yellow flowers in summer and autumn. 'Variegatum' has white-edged leaves. 60cm (2ft).

SMILACINA
(False Solomon's seal)

These perennials are similar to Solomon's seal *(Polygonatum)* in habit and foliage, but each stem carries clusters of tiny starry flowers at its tip. Like Solomon's seal, *Smilacina* is ideal for those cool shady spots in shrub borders or woodland gardens.

HOW TO GROW

Grow in humus-rich, moisture-retentive but not wet soil, in partial shade. Plant in autumn or spring.

PROPAGATION

Divide carefully at planting time.

POPULAR SPECIES

S. racemosa (USA). This is the false spikenard; long pointed leaves to 15cm

▲ *Smilacina racemosa*

(6in); flowers white in plume-like clusters in late spring, followed by red fruits. 60–90cm (2–3ft).
S. stellata (W. USA). Known as the star-flowered lily-of-the-valley; leaves to 15cm (6in), long-pointed; white flowers in dense clusters, late spring; fruits green with black stripes, then dark red. 60cm (2ft).

SOLIDAGO
(Golden rod)

These are popular, easily grown, vigorous, clump-forming, herbaceous perennials. In the past they were so vigorous that they were considered to be weeds, but modern varieties are far more restrained. They produce sprays of yellow flowers in late summer and autumn and associate well with Michaelmas daisies *(Aster)* and with autumn-colouring shrubs.

HOW TO GROW

Grow in any moisture-retentive but not wet soil, in sun, although partial shade is tolerated. Plant in autumn or spring.

PROPAGATION

Lift and divide established clumps in the autumn or spring.

POPULAR SPECIES

S. canadensis (N. USA east of Rocky Mountains). Bright yellow flowers, summer to autumn. 1.5m (5ft).
S. virgaurea (Europe, Asia, N. Africa). Yellow flowers, summer to autumn. 30–75cm (1–2½ft). There are several dwarf forms, including 'Brachystachys' and *S.v. cambrica*.
    There are hybrid varieties which are recommended: 'Cloth of Gold', 45cm (1½ft), deep yellow; 'Crown of Rays', 60cm (2ft), bright yellow; 'Golden Thumb', ('Queenie', 'Tom Thumb'), 30cm (12in), bushy and neat, yellow-tinted foliage, yellow flowers; 'Goldenmosa', 75cm (2½ft), compact and bushy, mimosa-like sprays of flowers in bright yellow; 'Lemore', 75cm (2½ft), lemon to primrose-yellow flowers.
X Solidaster luteus (Aster hybridus luteus). A hybrid between *Solidago* and *Aster,* but favouring aster in general appearance. Large heads of small, yellow, daisy-like flowers, summer to autumn.
60–75cm (2–2½ft).

▼ *Solidago virgaurea cambrica*

S. byzantina (S. lanata, S. olympica) (S.W. Asia to European Turkey). Popularly known as bunny's ears, lamb's ears, lamb's lugs, lamb's tongue. Mat-forming perennial with long, thick white woolly leaves; erect flowering stems to 30–45cm (1–1½ft) bearing purple flowers in summer. Even better for ground cover is the non-flowering 'Silver Carpet'.

S. grandiflora (Betonica grandiflora, Betonica macrantha) (Caucasus). Clump-forming; mauve-purple flowers in summer. 45–60cm (1½–2ft). 'Robusta' is more vigorous with richer-toned flowers.

▲ *Solidago* 'Crown of Rays'

▲ *Stachys byzantina* 'Silver Carpet'

▼ *Stachys grandiflora*

STACHYS
(Woundwort)

Of the many species of this genus, two are very different-looking plants: *S. byzantina*, a ground-cover plant with white woolly foliage (contrasting superbly with many plants, especially purple-leaved shrubs); and a superb herbaceous-border plant, *S. grandiflora*, which is a tall clump-forming plant.

HOW TO GROW

Grow in any well-drained soil in a sunny position. Plant in autumn or spring.

PROPAGATION

Divide established plants at planting time.

▲ *Stipa gigantea*

STIPA
(Feather grass)

These are tufted to clump-forming
ornamental grasses with slender leaves
and dainty 'clouds' of flowers in summer.
They are ideal for mixed and herbaceous
borders, and for growing in gravel areas.

HOW TO GROW
Grow in any well-drained soil in a sunny spot.
Plant in autumn or spring.

PROPAGATION
Lift and divide established clumps in the
autumn or spring.

POPULAR SPECIES
*S. calamagrostis (Achnatherum
calamagrostis)* (C. and E. Europe). Rolled,
rush-like leaves; silky silvery flowers,
summer. 1m (3ft).
S. gigantea (Spain, Portugal, Morocco).
Leaves to 75cm (2½ft), yellow hairy flowers
in summer. 1.5–2m (5–6ft).
S. pennata (C. to S.E. Europe). Known as
the common feather grass; leaves very
slender, rolled; silvery, silky, feathery,
flowers, summer. 60–90cm (2–3ft).

▲ *Stokesia laevis*

STOKESIA
(Stokes' aster)

This is an invaluable evergreen perennial
for herbaceous or mixed borders, and
herbaceous island beds, flowering in
summer and autumn. It has an extremely
long flowering period.

HOW TO GROW
Grow in fertile, well-drained soil in full sun.
Plant in autumn or spring.

PROPAGATION
Lift and divide established clumps during
the spring.

POPULAR SPECIES
S. laevis (S. cyanea) (S.E. USA). A clump-
forming perennial with 5–10cm (2–4in) wide,
somewhat cornflower-like flower heads in
lavender-blue. Varieties with white, creamy-
yellow, blue or purple flowers are
sometimes available. 'Blue Star', with light
blue flowers, is quite well known.

SYMPHYTUM
(Comfrey)

These are clump-forming perennials which
usually spread by rhizomes (underground
stems) and often have rough-textured leaves
and clusters of tubular to funnel-shaped
flowers in spring and summer. They make
quite good ground cover and can therefore

be drifted among shrubs or used in woodland gardens. They are also suitable for herbaceous borders, island beds and for cottage-garden planting schems.

HOW TO GROW

Grow in any reasonably fertile, moisture-retentive soil in sun or partial shade. Indeed, they are very easy-going plants. Plant in autumn or spring.

PROPAGATION

Divide established clumps at planting time. Take cuttings in winter and root under glass.

POPULAR SPECIES

S. caucasicum (Caucasus). Softly hairy all over; leaves up to 20cm (8in) long; red-purple flowers, turning sky-blue. 60cm (2ft).
S. grandiflorum (Caucasus). Slender,

forming leafy mats or colonies, spreading by rhizomes; cream flowers in spring, then on and off until summer. 30cm (12in). Useful ground cover beneath trees where the soil is not too dry.
S. officinale (Europe to W. Siberia and Turkey). This is the common comfrey; tuberous roots; leaves up to 25cm (10in) long; flowers white, cream, purple or pink, early summer. 45–120cm (1½–4ft). Suitable for a wild garden.
S. rubrum (possibly a hybrid). Has a spreading habit; crimson flowers in early summer. 45cm (1½ft).
S. × uplandicum. A varied assemblage of hybrids, similar in overall appearance to *S. offinale,* one of the parents. Flowers usually in shades of blue and purple, summer. The variety 'Variegatum' has grey-green, cream-edged leaves.

▼ *Symphytum caucasicum*

T

TELLIMA
(Fringecup)

This prennial has evergreen foliage and is useful for ground cover in shrub or mixed borders or in woodland gardens.

HOW TO GROW
Tellima should be grown in moisture-retentive but well-drained soil in sun or shade. Plant in autumn or spring.

PROPAGATION
Lift and divide established clumps in the autumn or spring.

POPULAR SPECIES
T. grandiflora (T. odorata) (Alaska to California). This is the only species. A clump-forming plant with rounded, tooth-edged, hairy leaves on long stalks; tiny urn-shaped flowers on erect stems to 60cm (2ft) tall; green-white, reddening with age, late spring and summer. Variety 'Purpurea' ('Rubra') has purple-red winter foliage and pink-flushed flowers.

▼ *Tellima grandiflora*

TEUCRIUM
(Germander)

These are really sub-shrubs rather than perennials but are included here for convenience. The dwarf plants described here are suitable for rock gardens or for the front of mixed or herbaceous borders. They are evergreen and produce whorls of small tubular flowers.

HOW TO GROW
Germanders need a well-drained soil in full sun. Plant in autumn or spring.

PROPAGATION
Divide or sow seeds in spring, or take cuttings and root in the summer.

POPULAR SPECIES
T. chamaedrys (Europe, S.W. Asia). Glossy deep green leaves; and pale to deep rosy-purple flowers in late summer. 30cm (12in) or more.
T. polium (S. Europe, S.W. Asia). Erect or sprawling stems, which are grey-white or yellow and downy; grey or white downy leaves; heads of white or red flowers in summer. 20–45cm (8–18in).

▼ *Teucrium chamaedrys*

THALICTRUM
(Meadow rue)

The clump-forming thalictrums are attractive in all their parts. They have delicate fern-like foliage and, in summer, large but dainty sprays of tiny flowers. The meadow rues are suited to both herbaceous and shrub borders and do not look out of place, either, on the edge of a woodland garden. Some are traditionally grown in cottage gardens.

HOW TO GROW

Meadow rues like a humus-rich, moisture-retentive but well-drained soil in sun or partial shade. Add plenty of peat or leaf-mould before planting. Plant in the autumn or spring.

PROPAGATION

Divide at planting time; take basal cuttings in spring and root under glass; sow seed as soon as ripe.

POPULAR SPECIES

T. aquilegifolium (E. and C. Europe, N. Asia). Blue-grey, shiny leaves, and white and lilac, purple or pink flowers, early summer. 60–90cm (2–3ft).
T. delavayi (W. China). Flowers mauve to lilac and yellow, summer. 75–150cm (2½–5ft). The variety *T.d.* 'Hewitt's Double' (*T. dipterocarpum* 'Hewitt's Double'), has fully double, lilac flowers.
T. dipterocarpum (W. China). Almost indistinguishable from *T. delavayi* (small botanical differences).
T. flavum (Europe, temperate Asia). Known as the common meadow rue; grows from rhizomes, forming colonies; well-branched flower heads bear white and bright yellow flowers, late summer. 1–1.5m (3–5ft). *T.f. glaucum* (*T.f. speciosum, T. glaucum, T. speciosum*) is more robust than the species, with grey-green foliage.
T. rochebrunianum (*T. rocquebrunianum*) (Japan). Tall, purple stems, and large, well-branched flower heads bearing pale purple flowers in late summer. 75–100cm (2½–3ft) high.

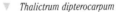
Thalictrum aquilegifolium
Thalictrum dipterocarpum

▲ *Thymus × citriodorus* 'Aureus'

▲ *Thymus praecox arcticus* 'Coccineus'

THYMUS
(Thyme)

The thymes are shrubs and sub-shrubs but to most people they really look like perennials, especially the carpeting thymes, so it is convenient to deal with them here. The carpeting thymes, with their aromatic foliage, are ideal for planting in gaps in crazy or random-stone paving, for edging beds and borders and even for growing on rock gardens. No cottage garden should be without thymes creeping over the edge of the path.

HOW TO GROW

Grow in any well-drained soil in full sun. Plant in autumn or spring.

PROPAGATION

Divide or sow seed in spring; take cuttings and root in early or late summer.

POPULAR SPECIES

T. × citriodorus (T. pulegioides × T. vulgaris). This is the lemon-scented thyme; a spreading bush 10–30cm (4–12in) tall; lemon-scented leaves. Several varieties: 'Argenteus' *(T. vulgaris* 'Argenteus'), leaves white-variegated; 'Aureus' *(T. vulgaris* 'Aureus'), leaves yellow.

T. praecox (Europe). Mat-forming, 5–10cm (2–4in) tall; flowers in shades of purple, in great profusion. Commonly grown is *T. p. arcticus (T. drucei, T. serpyllum)*, with flowers of variable colour: varieties include 'Albus', pale foliage and white flowers; 'Annie Hall', flesh-pink; 'Coccineus' *(T. coccineus)*, dark foliage, crimson flowers; 'Pink Chintz', salmon-pink.

T. pseudolanuginosus (T. lanuginosus) (origin unknown). Mat-forming to 5cm (2in) tall; leaves very hairy; pink flowers.

TIARELLA

These evergreen perennials have rounded lobed leaves and spikes of small starry white flowers in summer. They are ideal for ground cover in woodland gardens or shrub borders.

HOW TO GROW

Tiarellas need a humus-rich soil so add plenty of peat or leaf-mould before planting. It should be moisture-retentive but well-drained (growth will be poor if the soil dries out in summer). Choose a position in partial

Tiarella cordifolia

PROPAGATION

Divide at planting time, or use the leaf plantlets in late summer to autumn – either peg them down to the soil or remove and treat as cuttings.

POPULAR SPECIES

T. menziesii (W. USA). Long-stalked, lobed, light green, hairy leaves; at the junction of the leaf stalk and blade a plantlet arises that roots and forms a new plant when the leaf touches the soil; small tubular green- and chocolate-purple flowers in summer. 45–60cm (1½–2ft) when in flower.

Tolmiea menziesii

shade. Plant in autumn or spring.

PROPAGATION

Lift and divide established clumps in the autumn or spring.

POPULAR SPECIES

T. cordifolia (N. America). Known as the foamflower; forms wide mats; leaves often flecked deep maroon, flushed red-bronze in winter; white or pink-tinted flowers. One of the best species for ground cover. 15–30cm (6–12in).
T. trifoliata (N.W. USA). Clump-forming; flowers white, pink-tinted in bud. Up to 45cm (1½ft) high.

TOLMIEA
(Pick-a-back plant, youth-on-age)

This is the only species in the genus. It is a low-growing clump-forming evergreen perennial which makes useful ground cover in woodland gardens and shrub borders.

HOW TO GROW

Grow in any moderately fertile, moisture-retentive but well-drained soil in partial shade. Plant in autumn or spring.

TRADESCANTIA
(Spiderwort)

The spiderworts are very popular herbaceous plants which flower over a long period in summer. They are suitable for herbaceous borders and beds and also combine well with shrubs in mixed or shrub borders. Traditionally they are planted in cottage gardens.

The foliage is grassy, quite broad and the flowers, on upright stems, are three-petalled. Tradescantias combine well with plants that have rounded or broad leaves, such as hostas and bergenias.

Tradescantia × *andersoniana* hybrid

HOW TO GROW

Grow in fertile, well-drained but moisture-retentive soil in sun or partial shade. Plant in autumn or spring.

PROPAGATION

Lift and divide established clumps in the autumn or spring.

POPULAR SPECIES

T. × *andersoniana* (better known as *T. virginiana)*. Vigorous, clump-forming, upright perennial with grassy foliage and fairly large flowers in shades of velvety blue to red-purple and white, in summer and autumn. There are numerous varieties including 'J.C. Weguelin', 45cm (1½ft), azure-blue; 'Osprey', 60cm (2ft), white with blue-bearded stamens; 'Purple Dome', 45cm (1½ft), rich purple; 'Rubra', 45cm (1½ft), deep rose-red.

T. virginiana (E. USA). This is the common spiderwort; clump-forming species with grassy foliage; blue, purple or pink flowers in summer. 30cm (12in). Plants listed under this name are usually *T.* × *andersoniana.*

TRILLIUM
(Wake-robin, birth-root, wood-lily)

The trilliums are choice woodland plants, yet easily grown elsewhere given the right conditions. If you do not have a woodland garden, then the next best place to grow trilliums is in a shrub border. These herbaceous plants carry their leaves and petals in threes and flower in spring to early summer.

HOW TO GROW

Grow in moisture-retentive yet well-drained, humus-rich soil in partial shade. Incorporate a good quantity of peat or leaf-mould into the soil before planting. Plant when dormant (late summer/autumn to late winter).

PROPAGATION

Divide at planting time, or sow from seed as soon as ripe.

POPULAR SPECIES

T. catesbaei (T. nervosum, T. stylosum) (S.E. USA). Pale to deep pink flowers. 30–45cm (1–1½ft).
T. erectum (E. USA). This plant is variously known as birth-root, squawroot, stinking Benjamin; flowers crimson to purple, brown, sometimes white (*T.e.* 'Album') or green, held upright. 30–45cm (1–1½ft).
T.e. 'Flavum' *(T.e. luteum, T. flavum),* has yellow flowers.
T. grandiflorum (E. USA). Known as the wake-robin, or common wood-lily; a robust species with large leaves and flowers; blooms white, ageing to pink. 30–45cm (1–1½ft). Varieties: 'Plenum' with double flowers; and 'Variegatum' with green-striped petals.
T. ovatum (T. californicum) (W. USA). White flowers, ageing to pink. 20–30cm (8–12in).
T. sessile (E. USA). Commonly called

△ *Trillium grandiflorum*

toadshade, or wake-robin; leaves have a mottled pattern of pale and dark green; flowers maroon to yellow-green. 20–30cm (8–12in).

T. undulatum (E. USA). Painted wood-lily; flowers have wavy petals, white with a basal horseshoe of red-purple. 30cm (12in).

▽ *Trillium ovatum*

TROLLIUS
(Globe flower)

The globe flowers are very showy herbaceous perennials for moist places and even for growing in bog gardens. They form clumps and in summer (usually early summer) produce large, mainly globe-shaped flowers in profusion. The flowers are usually in shades of yellow. These plants look superb with moisture-loving irises.

HOW TO GROW

Grow in moist soil or preferably a bog garden, in sun, or partial shade. Plant in autumn or early spring.

PROPAGATION

Lift and divide established clumps in the autumn or spring.

▲ *Trollius × cultorum* 'Earliest of All'

▼ *Trollius europaeus* 'Superbus'

V

VALERIANA
(Valerian)

The most attractive of the valerians is *V. phu* 'Aurea' which has the most beautiful, bright yellow, young foliage in the spring which contrasts superbly with other spring perennials such as pulmonarias, and with dwarf bulbs.

▼ *Valeriana montana*

POPULAR SPECIES

T. × cultorum (T. × hybridus). Group of garden varieties mainly derived from *T. europaeus*, the similar but smaller *T. asiaticus* and the more robust *T. chinensis*. They resemble *T. europaeus* but generally have larger flowers and are more robust. 60cm (2ft) or more. Among the best are 'Alabaster', pale primrose; 'Canary Bird', large lemon-yellow; 'Commander-in-Chief', very large deep orange; 'Earliest of All', lemon-yellow, late spring; 'Golden Queen', golden-orange; 'Orange Princess', orange-yellow; 'Salamanda', deep orange.

T. europaeus (Europe to Caucasus and Canada). Attractive deeply lobed leaves; large pale yellow flowers. 60cm (2ft). The variety 'Superbus', up to 75cm (2½ft) tall, has clear lemon-yellow flowers.

T. yunnanensis (T. pumilus yunnanensis) (W. China). Lobed broadly and sharply toothed leaves; large golden-yellow flowers opening flat. 60cm (2ft).

HOW TO GROW

Grow in fertile, well-drained soil in sun or partial shade. Plant in autumn or spring.

▼ *Valeriana phu* 'Aurea'

PROPAGATION

Divide or take basal cuttings and plant during the spring.

POPULAR SPECIES

V. montana (Pyrenees, Alps, Apennines). Known as the mountain valerian; this is a low clump-forming plant with heads of pink or white flowers, on upright stems, in spring. It grows up to 45cm (1½ft), although a dwarf, broad-leaved form is usually grown, up to 10cm (4in) tall; this dwarf plant is ideal for all kinds of rock gardens.
V. phu (Caucasus). Clump-forming species with sprays of tiny white flowers in late summer. The variety 'Aurea' is usually grown, with bright yellow young foliage. 30cm (12in).

VERATRUM
(False hellebore, helleborine)

These are robust, clump-forming herbaceous perennials grown mainly for their distinctive foliage. They have boldly ribbed and pleated long leaves and generally large, dense heads of small flowers in summer. They associate particularly well with shrubs and are therefore best planted in shrub borders or woodland gardens.

HOW TO GROW

Grow in moisture-retentive, humus-rich soil (add plenty of peat or leaf-mould before planting) in sun or partial shade. Plant in autumn or spring.

Veratrum album

PROPAGATION

Lift and divide established clumps carefully in late winter.

POPULAR SPECIES

V. album (Europe, temperate Asia). Known as the white false hellebore; 30cm (12in) long basal leaves; palest green, almost white flowers in 60cm (2ft) long heads. Up to 2m (6ft) high.
V. nigrum (C. and S.E. Europe, N. Asia). This is the black false hellebore; basal leaves to 30cm (12in); maroon flowers. 1.2–2m (4–6ft) high.

VERBASCUM
(Mullein)

The perennial or biennial verbascums are stately border plants with bold spikes of flowers in summer. They are invaluable in herbaceous or shrub borders for providing contrast in shape and texture. They form a rosette of foliage from the centre of which the flower stem emerges. The leaves are usually very attractive, being covered in 'felt' or hairs.

HOW TO GROW

Grow in any well-drained soil in sun. Plant in autumn or spring.

PROPAGATION

Sow from seed or divide perennials during the spring.

POPULAR SPECIES

V. bombyciferum (V. broussa) (Turkey). Biennial (dies after flowering); white-felted basal leaves; bright yellow flowers in summer. 2m (6ft).
V. chaixii (S.C. and E. Europe, including N.E. Spain). Perennial; grey hairy basal leaves; yellow flowers with purple anthers, in summer. The variety 'Album' has white flowers. 45–90cm (1½–3ft).
V. olympicum (reputedly from Greece). Biennial or perennial; white woolly basal leaves; bright rich yellow flowers. 1.5–2.5m (5–8ft) high.
V. phoeniceum (E.C. and S.E. Europe,

Verbascum phoeniceum 'Gainsborough'

Asia). This is the purple mullein; perennial; dark green basal leaves; flowers in shades of purple, rarely yellow, from summer to early autumn. 90–120cm (3–4ft). The following varieties are recommended: 'Bridal Bouquet', white; 'Cotswold Beauty', biscuit, lilac anthers; 'Cotswold Queen', terracotta'; 'Gainsborough', primrose-yellow; 'Hartleyi', biscuit-yellow, suffused plum-purple; 'Pink Domino', with dusky pink flowers.
V. thapsus (Europe, Asia). Called the common mullein, or flannel plant; biennial; grey or white woolly basal leaves; yellow flowers, early to late summer. 1.2–2m (4–6ft) high.
V. vernale (not a wild species). Perennial; very branching flower stem; flowers vivid yellow. 2m (6ft).

Verbascum bombyciferum

Verbascum vernale

VERONICA
(Speedwell)

These are very popular and highly recommended herbaceous perennials for herbaceous or mixed borders, flowering over a long period in summer. They have small saucer-shaped flowers carried in spikes and the usual colour is blue, ranging from a pale blue to a deep lavender blue.

HOW TO GROW
The speedwells grow best in fertile, well-drained soil in full sun. Plant in the autumn or spring.

PROPAGATION
Lift and divide established clumps in the autumn or spring.

POPULAR SPECIES
V. austriaca (V. latifolia) (Europe). Varieties of *V.a. teucrium (V. teucrium)*, are usually grown, such as 'Crater Lake Blue', deep blue, 30cm (12in); 'Pavane', pink, 60cm

Veronica virginica 'Rosea'

Veronica a. teucrium 'Shirley Blue'

▲ *Veronica longifolia* 'Foerster's Blue'

(2ft); 'Shirley Blue', brilliant blue, 20cm (8in); and 'Trehane', deep blue, 20cm (8in).
V. gentianoides (Crimea, Caucasus). Palest blue flowers with darker veins, early summer. 30–45cm (1–1½ft). *V.g. 'Variegata'* has white-splashed leaves.
V. longifolia (N.E. and C. Europe, Asia). Lilac or blue flowers in long spikes, summer. 60–120cm (2–4ft). Varieties include *V. l. exaltata* (Siberia), clear pale blue, 1.2m (4ft); and 'Foerster's Blue', deep blue, 60cm (2ft).
V. spicata (Europe, Asia). Commonly known as the spiked speedwell; spikes of blue flowers in late summer. 30–60cm (1–2ft). Varieties include 'Barcarolle', rich pink, 45cm (1½ft); 'Blue Fox', bright lavender-blue, 45cm (1½ft); *V.s. incana (V. incana)*, leaves silvery-white, hairy, flowers deep blue, 30cm (12in); 'Red Fox', crimson; 'Snow White', pure white.
V. virginica (Veronicastrum virginica) (E. USA). Culver's root, blackroot; palest blue or lilac-pink flowers in late summer to autumn. 1.2–2m (4–6ft). The variety 'Alba' has white flowers.

VIOLA
(Violet)

The violas are well-loved, 'old-fashioned' garden perennials, much used in cottage gardens. Today, they should be in every cottage-style garden and are useful, too, for edging beds and borders. Violas are also suited to woodland gardens and to being drifted through shrubs in mixed borders.

Most of the violas are clump-forming plants of very dwarf habit. The flowers are distinctive in shape, composed of five petals, the upper two often longer and upright and the lower one usually broader.

HOW TO GROW
Violas like a humus-rich soil so work in plenty of peat or leaf-mould before planting. The soil should be well-drained, yet not prone to drying out. Violas thrive in partial shade but also take full sun. Plant in autumn or spring.

PROPAGATION
Sow seed or divide in spring; or take basal cuttings in late summer and root in a garden frame.

POPULAR SPECIES
V. aetolica (V. saxatilis aetolica) (Balkan Peninsula). Similar to *V. tricolor*, but more prostrate and up to 10cm (4in) tall; bright yellow flowers, spring and early summer.
V. cornuta (Pyrenees). Small, clump-forming, spreads by rhizomes; flowers fragrant, violet-purple to lilac, summer. 15cm (6in). Variety 'Alba' has white flowers.
V. cucullata (E. USA). Spreads by thick fleshy rhizomes (underground stems); violet-purple flowers, spring to summer. 10cm (4in).
V. gracilis (Balkan Peninsula). Mat-forming; yellow or violet flowers, spring and early summer. 10–15cm (4–6in). Varieties include 'Major', with deep purple flowers; and 'Moonlight', pale yellow.
V. labradorica (N. USA to Greenland). Mat-forming; light purple-blue flowers in spring. 10cm (4in). The leaves of 'Purpurea' are suffused deep purple.

Viola labradorica 'Purpurea'

V. odorata (Europe, N. Africa, Asia). This is the sweet violet; mat-forming species; fragrant violet-purple flowers from early spring to summer. 10cm (4in). A variable species; many varieties have been recorded in shades of violet, purple and lilac, some much larger and double. Varieties include 'Alba', white; 'Coeur d'Alsace', carmine-pink; 'Czar', large, deep violet-purple; 'Sulphurea', apricot-yellow and purple.

V. tricolor (Europe, Asia). Called the wild pansy, or heartsease; annual or short-lived tufted perennial; blue-violet or yellow flowers, often bi-coloured, spring to autumn. 15cm (6in) or more. The variety 'Bowles' Black' has black-purple flowers.

Viola cornuta 'Alba'

W

WALDSTEINIA

This is a mat-forming perennial, related to the strawberry, and looks something like it. It is an excellent ground-cover plant, for example among shrubs or on a bank.

HOW TO GROW

Grow in any well-drained but not dry soil in a sunny or partially shaded site. Plant in autumn or spring.

PROPAGATION

Lift and divide established mats in the autumn or spring.

POPULAR SPECIES

W. ternata (W. trifolia) (C. Europe to Siberia and Japan). This is generally the only species available. It is evergreen and forms mats up to 1m (3ft) or so wide by 10cm (4in) tall. Each leaf is composed of three leaflets; the yellow strawberry-like flowers, up to 2cm (¾in) wide, appear in clusters during spring and early summer.

Waldsteinia ternata

Z

ZANTEDESCHIA
(Arum lily, calla lily)

These impressive perennials have large, somewhat arrow-shaped leaves and large tubular flowers in summer (correctly called spathes). They grow from thick, fleshy, tuber-like rhizomes (underground stems). Only one species can be grown outdoors in areas that are subjected to frosts in winter,

and that is *Z. aethiopica.* It can be grown in borders, in association with shrubs, and also thrives in water up to 30cm (12in) deep.

HOW TO GROW

This plant needs a moisture-retentive soil and will also grow in water, in sun or partial shade. The site must be very sheltered. If grown in a border, mound over the crown in autumn with peat, sand or pulverized bark to protect it from frost. Remove this protection in spring. Given protection, or when grown in water, it will survive most winters. Plant in the spring.

▼ *Zantedeschia aethiopica*

PROPAGATION

Lift and divide established clumps very carefully at planting time. Remove offsets and root in spring.

POPULAR SPECIES

Z. aethiopica (Z. africana, Richardia africana) (S. Africa, naturalized in many frost-free areas of the world). The leaves are lustrous deep green; spathes white to creamy. 1m (3ft). The variety 'Crowborough' is more compact-growing than the species and reputedly hardier.

ZAUSCHNERIA
(Californian fuchsia)

These are somewhat fuchsia-like perennials with clusters of tubular flowers in the summer. They are ideal plants for hot dry parts of the garden, and associate particularly well with the many silver-leaved plants, which generally enjoy similar conditions.

 Zauschneria californica latifolia

▼ *Zauschneria cana*

HOW TO GROW

Grow in well-drained soil in sunny, sheltered sites. Plant in autumn or spring. In cold areas cover plants with cloches from late autumn onwards.

PROPAGATION

Take cuttings of basal non-flowering side shoots and root in late summer; or divide in the spring.

POPULAR SPECIES

Z. californica (Z. mexicana) (California, Mexico). Has rather a woody base and well-branched stems; long, thin, grey, downy leaves; bright red flowers, which bloom from late summer to mid autumn. 30–45cm (1–1½ft). The variety *Z.c. latifolia (Z.c. canescens)* has broader leaves than the species.
Z. cana (Z. microphylla) (California). Also has a woody base and similar to *Z. californica*, but leaves much narrower; the whole plant is downier, grey and hairy; bright red flowers, late summer to mid-autumn. 30–45cm (1–1½ft).

Cat Cranesbill

Geranium Regelii

June - July Bloom

Purple Coneflower

Echinacea

Purpurea

Full Sun -

Rosy Purple like

July - Mid Sept - clover

July - Mid Sept -

PICTURE ACKNOWLEDGEMENTS

A–Z Collection, B. Alfrieri, G. Beckett, Biofotos, Pat Brindley,
J. Cowley, Iris Hardwick, A. Huxley, Tania Midgley, Ray Proctor,
K. Scowen, Harry Smith Collection, Michael Warren.